# MAKING WOODEN
# Puzzle Playsets

# MAKING WOODEN
# Puzzle Playsets

## 10 Patterns to Carve, Scroll & Woodburn

CAROLEA HOWER

Fox Chapel
PUBLISHING

## Dedication

This book is dedicated to my son, Kevin Hower, whose computer skills, photography, and patience gave "life" to my patterns. To my husband, Kenneth Hower, for his unfailing support. And to my parents, Dale and Wilma White, who believed in me and started it all.

*Making Wooden Puzzle Playsets* is an original work, first published in 2015 by Fox Chapel Publishing Company, Inc. Portions of this book were originally published in *Woodcarving Illustrated* magazine and *Scroll Saw Woodworking & Crafts* magazine. The patterns contained herein are copyrighted by the author. Readers may make copies of these patterns for personal use. The patterns themselves, however, are not to be duplicated for resale or distribution under any circumstances. Any such copying is a violation of copyright law.

ISBN 978-1-56523-866-4

Library of Congress Cataloging-in-Publication Data

Hower, Carolea.
  Making wooden puzzle playsets / Carolea Hower.
     pages cm
  Includes index.
  ISBN 978-1-56523-866-4
  1. Wooden toy making. 2. Woodwork--Patterns 3. Wood-carved figurines. 4. Puzzles. I. Title.
  TT174.5.W6H69 2015
  745.592--dc23
                                    2015006010

To learn more about the other great books from Fox Chapel Publishing, or to find a retailer near you, call toll-free 800-457-9112 or visit us at *www.FoxChapelPublishing.com*.

**Note to Authors:** We are always looking for talented authors to write new books. Please send a brief letter describing your idea to Acquisition Editor, 1970 Broad Street, East Petersburg, PA 17520.

Printed in China
First printing

## About the Author

Carolea Hower grew up on a small dairy farm in Kansas. Today, she lives in a small south-central Kansas community, where she still actively farms with her husband, Ken. After working as a physical therapist for 44 years, Carolea retired and now "plays" with wood full time. (She notes that, before she retired, woodworking came after a day of work and her duties as a wife and mother, but before housework.) She also enjoys hunting and fishing with her husband.

Carolea's grandfather, an accomplished woodworker, taught her how to use a scroll saw when she was young. She focused on scrolling until 1992, when she saw a wonderfully carved Santa and decided to make one. She bought a book on Santa carving and has been carving ever since. She earned her first blue ribbon in a carving contest for her dragon "Smaug," and has since earned many more. She carves a variety of subjects; Santas and miniatures are her favorites. She often designs her carvings in Sculpey and relies on Ken to rough them out in wood using a small homemade duplicator; Carolea admits that she likes to carve details, but doesn't like the rough-out work.

Carolea says that as she carves or scrolls, she is transported back in time to experiences of her childhood. She enjoys remembering a slower, more gentle time.

# Contents

## PART 2: PROJECTS

18

Old MacDonald's Farm

50

Noah's Ark Two Ways

# Getting Started

Puzzle playsets are easy to make. You'll just need to make a few simple cuts using hand or power tools to shape the box and separate the pieces, glue and screw the box together, and then add the details to the puzzle pieces.

The pieces can be as simple or complex as you like. I usually woodburn the lines and paint the pieces. The woodburning helps to define the shapes and separate the paint colors, but you can leave it out if you prefer. I also enjoy shaping the pieces with carving tools. Like the woodburning, carving is entirely optional. You could also cut the pieces from hardwood, woodburn the details, and finish them with clear lacquer, or even cut the pieces from pine and give them to kids to color with markers or paint pens. The projects are intended to be fun and versatile.

This book includes two step-by-step projects: one shows the basic scrolling method and the other shows the carving method. All of the patterns can be used either way. These additional tips and tricks will help you get started on both styles of project.

## Choosing Wood

I use two types of wood for these puzzles: pine and basswood. I use pine for the scroll sawn puzzles. Pine is inexpensive, cuts easily, and shows the burned lines and finish well. However, pine can be difficult to carve, so I use basswood for the carved puzzles. Like pine, basswood is also light-colored and burns and accepts finishes well. Basswood is also fairly soft and has a regular grain pattern, which makes it very easy to carve.

You can buy pine at most lumberyards. You may need to visit a woodworking store or look online to buy basswood.

Pine

## Preparing the Wood

Cut the pieces to the rough dimensions listed at the beginning of each project. Most of the lumber I buy for these puzzles comes ¾" (19mm) thick. If you slice the wood in half, you're left with two ⅜" (10mm)-thick pieces, which I use for the bottom and doors on my puzzles. If you can't slice (or resaw) thick blanks, most wood supply places and craft stores sell ¼" (6mm)- to ⅜" (10mm)-thick blanks.

Sand the cut wood with progressively finer grits of sandpaper up to 120 grit. It's easier to remove imperfections from the wood now than after you cut the pieces.

Basswood

## Working with Patterns

To cut the box and puzzle pieces, you will need to attach paper patterns to the wood. There are several easy ways to attach the patterns.

- **SPRAY ADHESIVE OR GLUE STICK**: Photocopy the pattern. Cover the wood with painter's tape, which will lubricate the saw blade and make it easy to peel the pattern off. Spray adhesive or rub glue stick on the back of the pattern and smooth the pattern onto the tape. Cover the pattern with clear packing tape, if desired; this also helps to lubricate the blade.

- **SHELF PAPER**: Photocopy the pattern. Spray adhesive or rub glue stick on the back of the pattern and smooth the pattern onto the shiny side of the shelf paper. Cut the pieces apart, if necessary, and then peel the paper backing off the shelf paper and stick the pattern to the wood. The shelf paper both lubricates the blade and is easy to remove from the wood.

The patterns include detail lines that you will woodburn, carve, and/or paint. You will need to transfer these detail lines to the wood using one of the following methods. Remember to lift a corner of the pattern to make sure all of the pattern lines have transferred before you remove the pattern.

- **GRAPHITE PAPER**: Place graphite paper between the pattern and the blank, and use a pen to trace the lines onto the wood.

- **HEAT**: Make a photocopy of the pattern. Trim the excess paper off, and use tape to secure the pattern in position face-down on the wood. Make sure the tape does not cover any of the pattern lines. Rub the pattern lines with a hot iron or heated stamping tool.

- **ACETONE**: Make a photocopy of the pattern. Trim the excess paper off, and use tape to secure the pattern in position face-down on the wood. Apply a small amount of acetone to a rag, and rub the rag firmly over the back of the pattern. The acetone will soak through the paper and dissolve a small amount of the photocopy toner, which will transfer to the blank. Pure acetone can damage your skin and lungs, so use caution and work in a well-ventilated area.

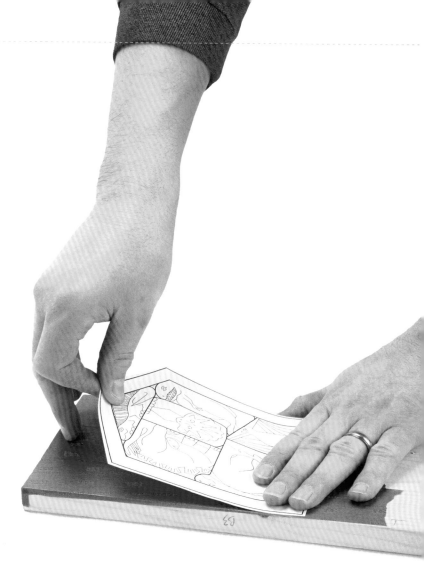

Apply spray adhesive to the back of the copy of the pattern and press it onto the tape-covered blank.

## Finishing the Puzzles

I generally stain the puzzle boxes and paint the pieces. Pine can be blotchy when you apply wood stain. To combat this, use a gel stain or apply a coat of white glue thinned heavily with water. This glue sizing helps the pine absorb the stain evenly.

I paint directly onto the raw wood using ordinary craft acrylics. I thin the paint slightly by mixing 1 part paint to 2 parts water. I do not dilute white or metallic paints.

Seal the completed puzzle box and pieces with spray lacquer or varnish, if desired.

# Tools & Supplies

While some projects require a few more tools, this basic tool kit will allow you to make most of the puzzles.

### Scroll Saw

I use a scroll saw with #7 reverse-tooth blades to cut the box and puzzle pieces. Not every scroll saw is created equally. When you reach the middle to high-quality saws, the differences are mostly personal preference. But, for an entry-level saw, look for a saw that will accept plain-end blades. You also want a saw that minimizes vibration. Many puzzle makers start with an entry-level saw, and upgrade to a more expensive saw later.

### Coping Saw or Fret Saw

You could also cut the puzzle pieces with a coping saw or fret saw. A coping saw uses pin-end blades, which require you to drill a larger blade-entry hole to accommodate the pins, but the saw and blades can be found in most hardware and home improvement stores. Fret saws use plain-end blades, like scroll saws, so you can drill smaller blade-entry holes, but they are usually only available from woodworking suppliers.

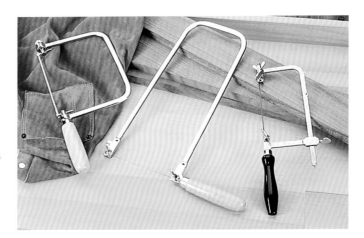

### Woodburner

There are two types of woodburners: hot wire and soldering iron (or solid tip). Either will work for this project. The hot-wire types have a greater assortment of tip shapes and heat up faster. The soldering-iron style burners are less expensive and hold their heat longer. With either machine, choose a skew or writing tip. If possible, choose a variable-temperature woodburning machine, which makes it easy to adjust the color of the lines you burn.

## Disc Sander and Belt Sander

Rather than worry about cutting the outside edges of the puzzles exactly on the line, I cut just outside the lines and sand up to the lines with a disc sander equipped with a 120-grit sanding disc. This tool quickly sands the layers all flush. I use a belt sander with a 1" (25mm)-wide belt to quickly round the edges of the puzzle pieces. The small belt lets me get into tight areas.

## Drill with Bits

I use a drill to make the blade-entry holes needed to cut the puzzle pieces free from the tray. The bits should be just large enough to feed the blades through; I use a #68 wire size bit. You can use a hand-held drill, but a drill press makes it easier to drill exactly vertical holes through the wood.

## Basic Carving Kit (optional)

You can carve these projects using traditional carving tools (knives, gouges, and V-tools), which are available at most woodworking suppliers. But, you could also use an inexpensive interchangeable carving kit, such as this one by X-Acto, or linoleum gouges (cutters), such as those made by Speedball. These kits feature disposable blades that come pre-sharpened and are available at most craft stores.

## Hand Tools

I use a 6" (152mm) square, a ruler, and a pencil to mark the locations of the hardware and to ensure the layers are all square. I use a hammer to drive brads and a Phillips screwdriver to attach the hinges and other hardware. I paint all of these projects with just three brushes: a ¼" (6mm)-wide shader, a ½" (13mm)-wide shader, and a #3 pointer.

# Basic Techniques

## Scrolling

Scroll saws allow you to cut intricate items using fine blades. By drilling a small blade-entry hole, you can also start a cut in the center of a piece of wood instead of having to cut in from the outside edge.

Most scroll saws have a variable speed setting. Cutting slowly might help you cut more accurately, but you can also push the wood against the blade too firmly and break the delicate blade. Cutting at a faster speed reduces blade breakage, but can make it more difficult to control the cuts. Practice cutting scrap wood that is similar to your project wood to get a feel for your saw and the blades. Adjust the speed as you cut until you find a tempo that works well for you.

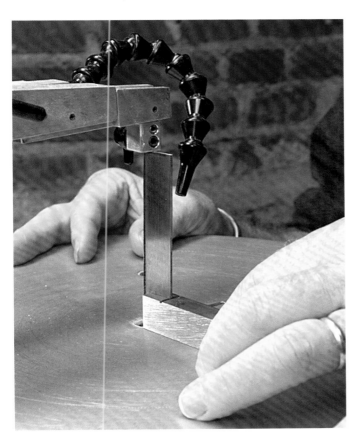

### SQUARING THE TABLE

Most scroll saws have an adjustable table that allows you to make cuts at different angles. There are times when you want the saw set at an angle, but most cutting is done with the blade perpendicular to the table. If the table is even slightly off square, the cuts will be angled and the puzzle won't fit together properly.

To square the table, place a small metal square, a right-angle tool, or an old credit card flat on the saw table against a tensioned blade. Adjust the table to form a 90° angle to the blade.

### BLADE TENSION

A blade that does not have enough tension will wander. It will also flex from side to side, making irregular or angled cuts. If you press too hard on a loose blade, it will usually snap. A blade that has too much tension is more susceptible to breaking and tends to pull out of the blade holders. In general, it is better to make the blade too tight than too loose.

Before inserting a blade, release the tension clamps or knobs. Clamp both ends of the blade into the blade holders and adjust the tension. Push on the blade with your finger. It should flex no more than ⅛" (3mm) forward, backward, or side-to-side.

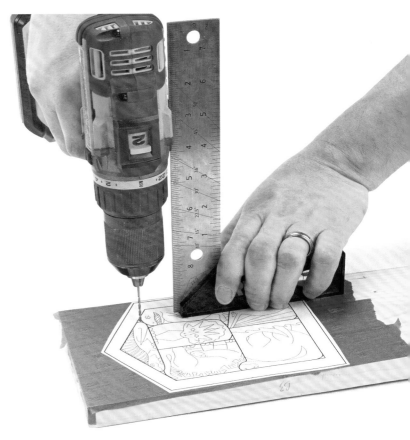

If you don't have a drill press, pair a handheld drill with a square to drill vertical blade-entry holes.

### BLADE-ENTRY HOLES

The blade-entry holes are marked on these patterns. Drill the holes exactly vertically through the wood (use a drill press or align a handheld drill with a metal square). Drill through the project wood into scrap wood to prevent tear-out on the back side of the project. If you have the space, use a larger bit to make it easier to thread the blades through. For thin veining cuts, use the smallest bit the blade will fit through.

### FOLLOWING PATTERN LINES

No matter how much you stray from the pattern lines, these puzzles will still fit together. This means you can really just start cutting without worrying about making mistakes. You may need to adjust the detail patterns slightly, but when the patterns have been removed, people will not know if you strayed from the lines.

### CUTTING TIGHT CORNERS

With practice, you can cut almost perfect 90° corners with a scroll saw just by spinning the wood. To practice this technique, cut into a piece of scrap wood about ½" (13mm), spin the wood, and cut back out along the line. Repeat the process until you can create just a tiny hole at the point where you spin the wood.

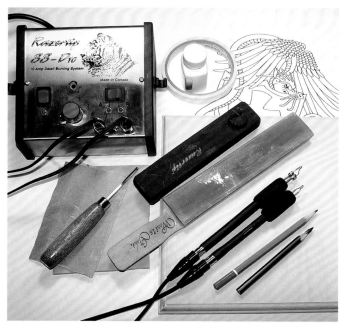

## Woodburning Basics

Woodburning along the pattern lines allows you to create interesting details on the puzzle pieces and box. The burned lines also keep paint from migrating from one area to another. Once you have a burner, pyrography is as easy as tracing along the lines.

### SELECTING TIPS

Once you settle on your burner (see page 10), the tip selection is up to you. I use a skew tip, but depending on your burner, a skew can slice, rather than burn, the lines. A writing tip also works well, but it doesn't burn as deeply as a skew does.

### SETTING THE TEMPERATURE

The trick to woodburning is to set the temperature of the burner correctly. If the burner is too hot, it will char the wood. Charred wood is unattractive, and it doesn't take a finish well. If the temperature isn't hot enough, the lines won't be dark enough to be visible. Most hot-wire burners have variable temperature settings, so it's easy to adjust the heat. Start low; it's better to burn a line twice than to char the wood.

Soldering-iron style, or solid-tip, burners often are not adjustable. These single-temperature burners are more challenging because they take a while to heat, and they cool slowly. If a single-temperature unit is running too hot, unplug it for a bit or doodle on a piece of scrap wood to get rid of some excess heat.

## MAINTAINING TIPS

Because you are burning wood, black carbon (like charcoal) will build up on the tip and interfere with how it burns the wood. Use a bit of fine-grit sandpaper or a razor blade to carefully remove the carbon buildup.

## BURNING SMOOTH LINES

Practice woodburning on scrap wood before you work on the project. Glide the tip down and lift it off smoothly, and keep it moving on the wood. If you hesitate with the tip on the wood, you will burn a blob or splotch in the line. Practice gliding, drawing, and lifting smoothly until you are comfortable with the movement.

Rub a woodburner tip on fine-grit sandpaper to carefully remove carbon buildup.

## FIXING MISTAKES

Once in a while you will stray from the line while burning. Use a razor blade to carefully scrape away the mistake.

## SAFETY

Although you should never have to deal with fire, woodburning does involve both heat and smoke. Protect yourself with a few simple measures.

- Work in a well-ventilated room. Use a fan, pointed away from your work, to draw the smoke away from your face.
- Turn the burner off when you're not working with it. It's easy to get distracted and forget it's on. This is especially important if you have children.
- Turn off the machine and use pliers to change tips. Put hot tips in a metal jar lid to cool.
- Puzzle pieces are small, so consider holding them with pliers while you burn the detail lines. You can also work on a gently tilted surface to keep your hand away from the heat of the burner.
- Never burn sealed or treated wood, manmade boards, MDF, or other bonded material. Burning these types of treated wood can release toxic fumes.

## Carving Basics

Add more detail to the puzzle box and pieces by carving along the pattern lines. You don't need to be an experienced carver or own special tools to carve (see page 12). When you carve, strop the blades a few times on a piece of leather to tune up the edge, and wear latex-dipped gardening gloves to protect your hands.

### WOOD GRAIN

The wood grain is visible as lines that run the length of the wood (see page 8). Before you start the project, carve some scrap wood. When you carve with the grain (downhill) or across the grain, you will get nice clean cuts. If you cut against the grain (uphill), the wood can split and break; at the least, you will tear the wood fibers and get a rough cut. If you have trouble when you are carving the pieces, turn the wood and carve from the other direction.

### BASIC KNIFE CUTS

You can carve the puzzles pieces with four basic cuts: the stop cut, the pushing cut, the V-shaped cut, and the paring cut.

**Stop Cut:** Stop cuts outline sections and make barriers for other cuts. To make a stop cut, hold the knife edge perpendicular with the wood, and cut straight in along the line. Repeat the cut several times to make it deeper.

**Pushing Cut:** Use push cuts to round sharp edges, to carve up to a stop cut to separate parts of the pattern, to make V-shaped cuts, or to create depth and dimension. Hold the knife in your dominant hand with your thumb at the back of the blade. Hold the wood in your other hand. Hold the knife at a slight angle with your carving thumb against the knife and your holding thumb braced against the carving thumb; carefully push the knife through the wood.

**V-shaped Cut:** V-shaped cuts outline and separate parts of the pattern. Cut in at an angle from one side. Then, cut in at the same angle from the other side. Position the knife so the cuts will meet in the center, forming a V-shaped trough.

**Paring Cut:** This cut is useful for shaving wood away and, depending on the grain direction and shape of the pieces, it may be the only way to get a clean cut without tearing the wood fibers. However, use this cut sparingly, because you'll be cutting towards your thumb. Hold the knife in your dominant hand with the knife edge facing toward your thumb. Position the knife on the wood where you want to make the cut, hook your thumb on the carving lower than the knife can cut, and pull the blade toward your thumb.

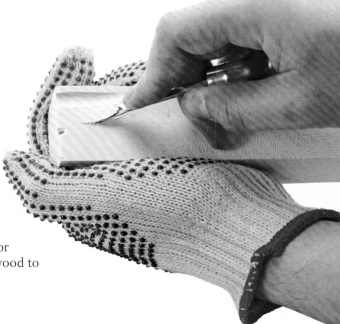

## USING GOUGES AND V-TOOLS

For these tools, simply push the tool into the wood to carve a trough or groove. Make shallow cuts, and keep the edges of the tool out of the wood to keep from tearing the wood fibers.

PROJECT:

# Old MacDonald's Farm

Having been raised on a Kansas farm, the farm puzzle was a delight for me to design. Although our farm was foremost a dairy farm, my folks always kept horses, sheep, pigs, chickens, ducks, geese, and a few turkeys to round out the cows. It was an all-around farm, and so is the farm in this puzzle.

## MATERIALS:

- Pine, ⅜" (10mm) thick: front A, back C, 2 each 6" x 7" (152mm x 178mm)
- Basswood, ⅝" to ¾" (16mm to 19mm) thick: center B, 6" x 7" (152mm x 178mm)
- Acetone or graphite paper
- Wire brads: #19 by 1" (25mm)
- Brass hinges: 4 each ¾" x ¾" (19mm x 19mm)
- Brass-plated hasp: ¾" x 1⅞" (19mm x 48mm)
- Brass screws: 20 each #1 by ⅜" (10mm)
- Stain: Minwax special walnut 224
- Sandpaper: 120 grit
- Tape: clear double-sided
- Round toothpicks
- Acrylic paint

1 **Transfer the patterns to the blanks.** Use your chosen method (see page 9). If you transfer the pattern with graphite paper, your project will be a mirror image of mine. Cut the perimeters of all three pieces. Cut on the center line to separate the doors.

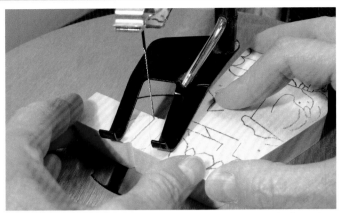

2 **Cut the puzzle pieces.** Drill a blade-entry hole where indicated on the center blank (B) and cut around the perimeter of the puzzle pieces. Set the puzzle frame aside and cut the puzzle pieces apart.

3 **Add the detail patterns.** Hand-sand the edges of each puzzle piece. Transfer the additional detail patterns to the sides and back of each piece.

4 **Sand the pieces.** I use a 1" (25mm)-wide belt sander equipped with a 120-grit belt to round all of the sharp corners. Then, hand-sand the edges of the pieces with 120-grit sandpaper.

5 **Woodburn the details.** Use a skew tip or a writing tip in your woodburner to burn deep lines along all of the transferred details. The deeply burned lines keep the paints from bleeding and add contrast to the stained barn scene. You do not need to burn past the gray puzzle frame alignment line.

6 **Assemble the box.** Attach the barn back (C) to the puzzle frame (the outside of B) with ¾" (19mm)-long brads. Use the gray puzzle frame alignment line as a guide. Attach the doors (A) to the puzzle frame (B) with double-sided tape. Press the doors firmly down onto the tape.

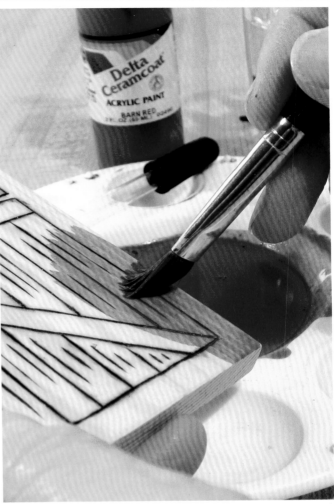

**7** **Sand the outside of the puzzle.** Sand the perimeter of the assembly with a disc sander equipped with a 120-grit disc. Sand until all three layers are flush on all sides. Use a 6" (152mm)-long square to make sure the sides are square with the bottom. Then, sand off any sharp corners.

**8** **Attach the hinges.** With the doors taped in place, attach the hinges with small screws. Use a thin knife blade to separate the tape securing the doors to the puzzle frame and remove the tape. Check to make sure the doors open freely. Remove the doors from the hinges, but leave the hinges attached to the puzzle frame. Sand the inside edges of the doors if needed.

**9** **Finish the doors.** Transfer the detail lines to the front and back of the doors and burn in the lines using a skew tip. Use the center pattern (B) to transfer the puzzle solution onto the back of the barn and burn those lines. Dilute 1 part barn red acrylic paint with 2 parts water to create a wash. Apply this wash to the doors. Stain the rest of the barn assembly.

**10** **Paint the pieces.** Paint the puzzle pieces with acrylic paint washes using 1 part paint to 2 parts water. Do not dilute the white or metallic paint. To add the highlights to the dog's eyes, apply a small amount of white to the eye using the tip of a round toothpick.

**11** **Attach the latch.** Reattach the doors to the hinges. Mark the location of the latch and install the latch. Seal the completed puzzle with spray lacquer or spray varnish if desired.

### PIG
- **Body:** Pink[1]
- **Hooves:** Black[1]

### DOG
- **Body:** Black[1]
- **Paws, tail tip, face, chest:** White[1]
- **Tongue:** Tompte red[1]

### CAT
- **Body:** Golden yellow[2]
- **Face, chest, paws, tail tip:** White[1]
- **Nose:** Pink[1]

### FARMER
- **Overalls, hat:** Copen blue[1]
- **Shirt:** Tompte red[1]
- **Hair, pitchfork handle:** Spice brown[1]
- **Pitchfork tines:** Aluminum[2]
- **Shoes:** Black[1]
- **Face, hands:** Flesh[1]

### TRACTOR
- **Body:** Christmas green[1]
- **Wheels, rims:** Bright yellow[3], black[1]
- **Axles, radiator, steering wheel:** Aluminum[2]
- **Exhaust pipe:** Black[1]
- **Ground:** Spice brown[1]

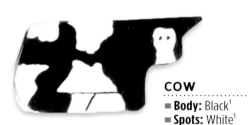

### COW
- **Body:** Black[1]
- **Spots:** White[1]

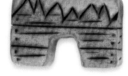

### MANGER
- **Box:** Spice brown[1]
- **Straw:** Golden yellow[2]

### HEN
- **Body:** Medium gray[2] with white[1] accents
- **Bill:** Bright yellow[3]
- **Wattles, comb:** Tompte red[1]
- **Eggs:** Oyster white[1]
- **Crate:** Spice brown[1]

### HORSE
- **Body:** Spice brown[1]
- **Mane, tail:** Bambi brown[1]

### ROOSTER
- **Body, feather trim:** Medium gray[2], metallic copper[2], topaz blue[1], Christmas green[1]
- **Wattles, comb:** Tompte red[1]
- **Bill:** Bright yellow[3]

### RABBIT
- **Body:** Medium gray[2]
- **Nose:** Pink[1]
- **Tail:** White[1]

1 Delta Ceramcoat
2 FolkArt
3 Apple Barrel
4 DecoArt

### SHEEP
- **Body:** Oyster white[1]
- **Horns:** Coffee bean[2]

### MILK CAN
- **All:** Aluminum[2]

### TURKEY
- **Body:** Burnt umber[1]
- **Feather trim:** Metallic copper[2], topaz blue[1], Christmas green[1]
- **Head, wattles:** Tompte red[1]
- **Bill:** Bright yellow[3]

### GOOSE & DUCK
- **Bodies:** White[1]
- **Bills:** Bright yellow[3]

## OLD MACDONALD'S FARM: Patterns

**Blade-entry hole**

**Old MacDonald's Farm Puzzle Pieces, Puzzle Frame, Back Woodburning Pattern (B)**

**Old MacDonald's Farm Puzzle Barn Doors (A)**

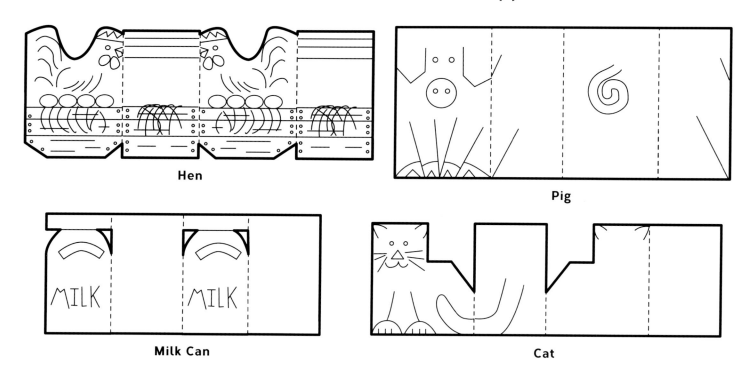

**Hen**

**Pig**

**Milk Can**

**Cat**

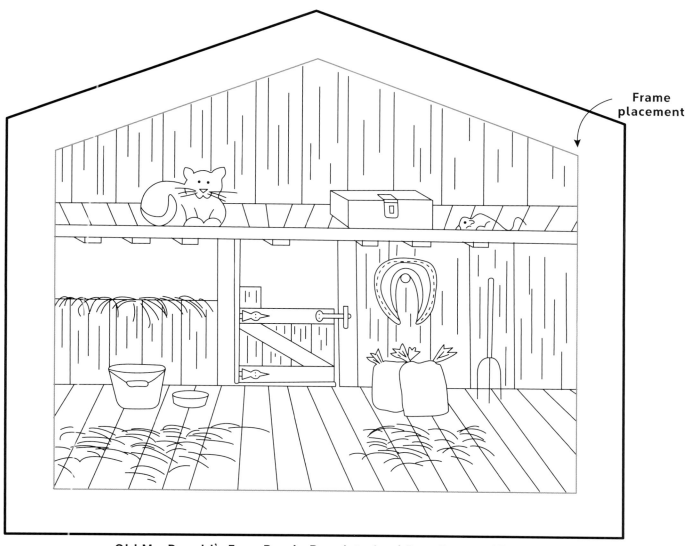

Frame placement

Old MacDonald's Farm Puzzle Barn Interior / Barn Bottom (C)

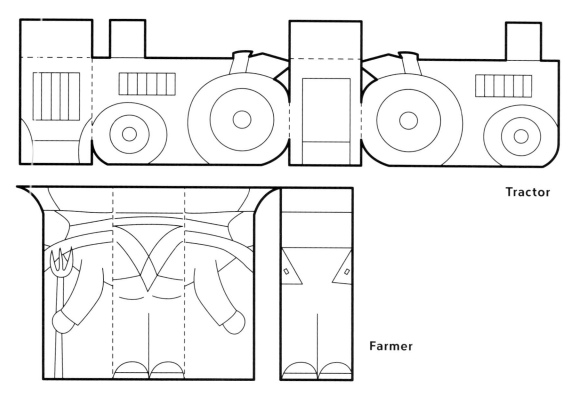

Tractor

Farmer

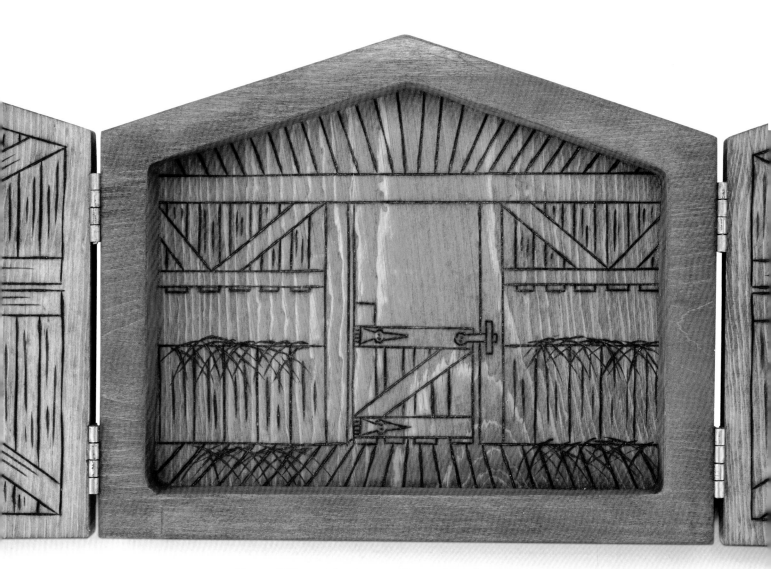

For a different look, woodburn this alternative design
onto the Old MacDonald's Farm Puzzle Barn Interior.

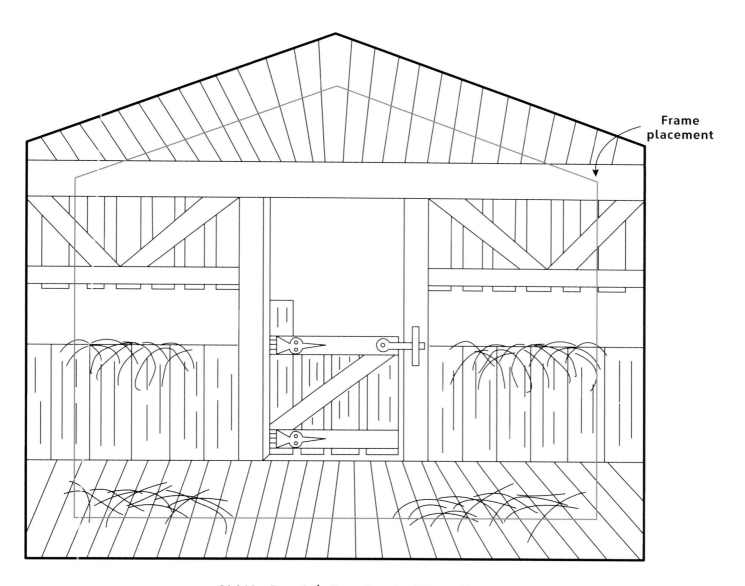

**Frame placement**

**Old MacDonald's Farm Puzzle Alternative**
**Barn Interior / Barn Bottom (C)**

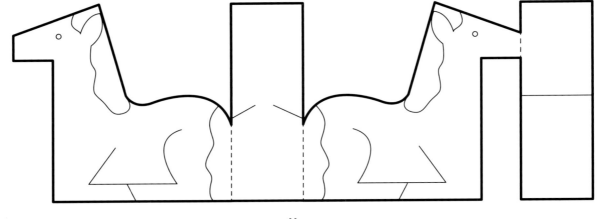

**Horse**

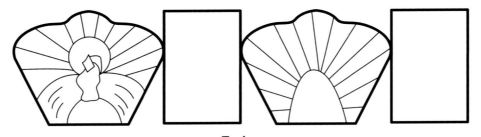

**Turkey**

**Duck**

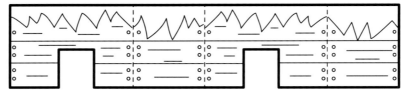

**Manger**

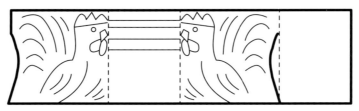

**Rooster**

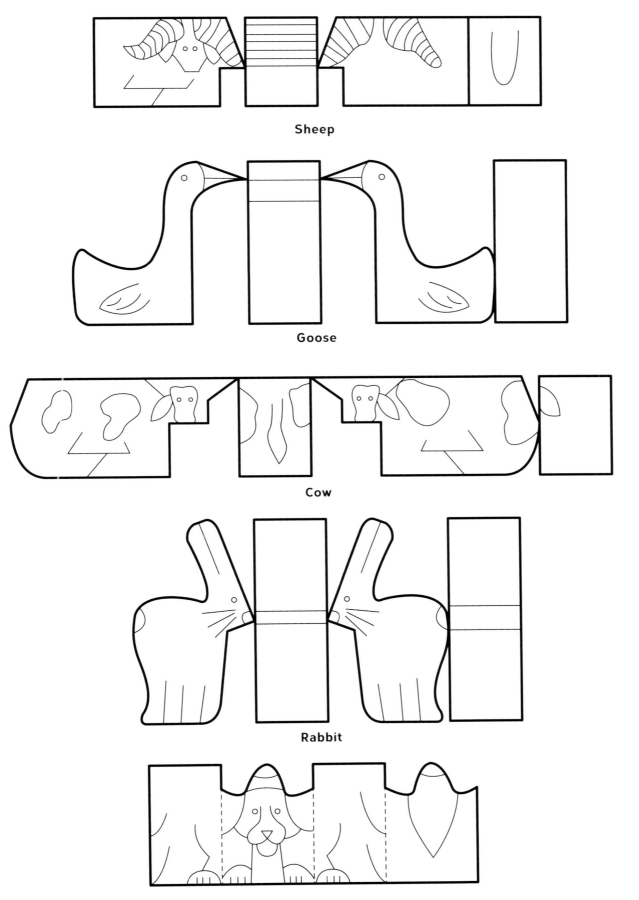

Sheep

Goose

Cow

Rabbit

Dog

PROJECT:

# Carved Dragon Castle

My son, Kevin, has liked dragons from the time the television movie "The Hobbit" was produced. He grew up reading anything "Middle Earth" and particularly liked the dragon "Smaug." Instead of just scroll sawing the dragon pieces, I decided to carve them 3-D for an extra special birthday present. In college, his major was computer graphics. After a request from me for some dragon drawings, he was quick to draw me a supply. He was very surprised when he opened the puzzle to find several of "his" dragons carved in 3-D.

The photos show carving tools available at most carving supply stores. You can carve these pieces using linoleum gouges (cutters) or inexpensive interchangeable carving kits, available at most craft stores. Use the techniques explained on page 20 to cut the perimeter of the three box pieces.

**MATERIALS:**

- Basswood, ⅜" (10mm) thick: front A, back C, 2 each 6" x 8" (152mm x 203mm)
- Basswood, 1½" (38mm) thick: center B, 6" x 8" (152mm x 203mm)
- Acetone or graphite paper
- Wire brads: #19 by 1" (25mm)
- Brass hinges: 4 each ¾" x ¾" (19mm x 19mm)
- Brass-plated hasp: ¾" x 1⅞" (19mm x 48mm)
- Brass screws: 20 each #1 by ⅜" (10mm)
- Stain: Minwax special walnut 224
- Sealer: water-based clear varnish
- Sandpaper: 120 grit
- Tape: clear double-sided
- Round toothpicks
- Acrylic paint
- Carving knife
- V-tool
- Nail set: 1⁄16" (2mm) dia.

**1 Cut the puzzle pieces.** Drill a ⅛" (3mm)-diameter blade-entry hole as indicated on pattern B, and use a scroll saw and #7 reverse-tooth blade to cut along the lines. Cut the puzzle into the individual pieces and set them aside.

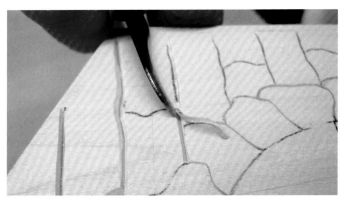

**2 Carve the rock wall lines.** Transfer the pattern details (C) to the front side of the box back piece. Carve V-shaped grooves around the rocks. Do not carve past the puzzle frame alignment line. Round the rock corners down into the grooves. Then, carve away the wood above the castle doors to create the sky background.

**3 Carve the doors (piece A).** Make stop cuts along the sides of the door hinges, and carve away the wood between the hinges. Use the micro V-tool to carve the spaces between the door boards. Use a sharpened 1/16" (2mm)-diameter nail set to press dots to resemble nail heads in the door hinges. If desired, transfer the outer door patterns to the front of the door piece and carve the rocks.

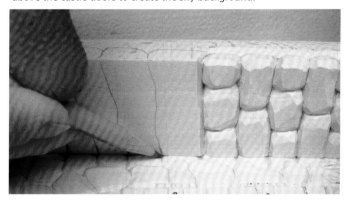

**4 Carve the puzzle frame (B).** Place the puzzle frame on the carved back. Mark the rock lines onto the sides and top based on the locations of the rocks carved into the back. Use the process explained in Step 2 to carve the rocks on the box sides.

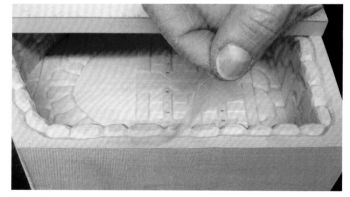

**5 Prepare to sand the box.** Attach the back to the box sides with 1" (25mm)-long brads. Mark the vertical line between the box doors. Cut along the line to separate the doors, and sand them smooth. Use double-sided tape to attach the doors to the box sides. Press the doors down firmly onto the tape.

**6 Sand the outside of the box.** Use a disc sander with a 120-grit disc to sand the perimeter of the assembly. Sand until all of the layers are flush on all of the sides. Use a 6" (152mm) square to make sure the sides are square with the bottom. Sand off any sharp edges.

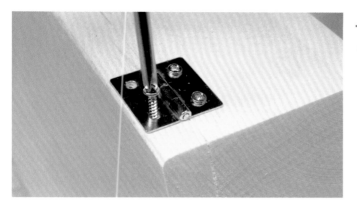

**7** **Finish assembling the box.** With the doors taped in place, attach the hinges with small screws. Use a thin knife blade to pry the doors open and remove the tape. Make sure the doors open freely. Remove the doors from the hinges, but leave the hinges attached to the sides. Sand the inside edges of the doors. Transfer the detail lines to the front and back of each door. Carve the door details with the technique used for the box back. Transfer the puzzle solution to the uncarved box back and woodburn along the lines.

---

**CARVED DRAGON CASTLE:** Carving a Dragon

**8** **Begin carving a dragon.** Transfer the detail patterns onto the back, front, top, and sides of each dragon piece. *Note: I am carving the blue dragon.* Remove the excess wood from around the wings, legs, head, and chest. Remove wood from between the wings. Then, shape the top and sides of the wings, legs, and wing veins.

**9** **Refine the carving.** Use a knife to carve the nostril notches. Redraw the backs of the legs, the tail, and the wing lines. Carve the wing lines. Round the chest with a knife. Mark and carve the top horns. Redraw the details on the head, legs, chest, top and tail scales, and the sides. Carve these details with a knife. Repeat the process on both wings.

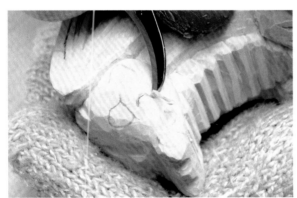

**10** **Carve the details.** Use a knife to carve the grooves between the toes, the grooves that separate the toes from the claws, and the grooves along the chest. Then, use the knife to make a stop cut along the top of the mouth and around the exposed tooth. Carve up to the stop cut to separate the top lip and the tooth from the mouth. Taper the top of the tooth to set it inside the mouth. Make stop cuts around the perimeters of the eyes and round them down to the stop cuts. Carve a wedge of wood out of the inside corner of each eye to set it into the face.

**11** **Finish carving the dragon.** Refine the head and chest, and make sure the cuts are clean. Carve the line for the chin. Draw the tail and back scales. Make a stop cut along the line and carve up to the line to set the scales in. Make a stop cut around the top wing knob, and carve up to it to separate the knob from the wing.

## Carving the Remaining Dragons

Use the same techniques to carve the other six dragons. The top red dragon's scales are carved against the grain of the wood. After carving them, use the flat side of a skew-shaped woodburning pen to remove any wood fuzzies around the cuts. Then, burn deep crack lines on the baby dragon egg; deep lines will prevent the paint from bleeding from one area to another during the painting process.

**12** **Paint the rocks.** Use a small brush to apply stain to the frame of the box and door frames next to the carved rocks. Paint the rocks with medium gray acrylic paint and allow it to dry. Thin 1 part black paint with 4 parts water. Working a few rows at a time, dampen the rocks with clean water and then dip the tip of a brush into the black wash and flow it into the cracks between the rocks, blending it into the sides. Apply additional coats to darken the cracks. Then, dilute 1 part white with 8 parts water. Use this wash to highlight the top of some of the rocks.

**13** **Finish painting the doors.** Paint the open castle doors, hinges, grass, and sky. Allow the paint to dry. Paint the birds with undiluted black and allow the paint to dry. Then, reattach the doors to the hinges. Mark the location of the latch and install it.

**14** **Basecoat the dragon.** Refer to the color chart or use your choice of colors to paint the dragon. Paint the entire dragon except the wing webbing, chest, and scales. Allow the paint to dry, and then paint the chest and wing webbing.

**15** **Shade the wings and chest.** Dampen the areas slightly with clean water. Pick up some dark shading color with the corner of a brush. From the edge of the area to be shaded, blend the paint from dark to light. Shade the entire piece, and then paint the claws, scales, fangs, and eyes. Paint a black iris in each eye and use a sharpened round toothpick to add white highlight dots. Outline the nose and mouth with black. Seal the completed puzzle with water-based clear varnish.

## PURPLE DRAGON

- **Body:** Passion purple[1]
- **Wings:** Bright yellow[3] shaded with orange[3]
- **Wing veins:** Violet pansy[2]
- **Scales and horns:** Metallic copper[2] and splendid gold[2]
- **Claws:** White[1] shaded with black[1]

## BOTTOM RED DRAGON

- **Body:** Alizaron crimson[4]
- **Horns, breastplate:** Bambi brown[1] shaded with dark brown[1]
- **Rocks:** Medium gray[2] shaded with black[1] and highlighted with white[1]
- **Claws:** Linen[2]

## BLUE DRAGON

- **Body:** Copenhagen blue[4]
- **Wings:** Light yellow[3] shaded with Copenhagen blue[4]
- **Scales, horns, and claws:** Metallic silver[2] and splendid gold[2]

## FULL GREEN DRAGON

- **Body:** Leaf green[1]
- **Wing veins:** Christmas green[1]
- **Breast plate:** Yellow[1] shaded with burnt umber[1]
- **Wings:** Linen[2] shaded with burnt umber[1]
- **Scales:** Metallic copper[2] and rich espresso[2]
- **Claws:** Linen[2]

## TOP RED DRAGON

- **Body:** Alizaron crimson[4]
- **Wing veins:** Black cherry[2]
- **Wings, breast plate:** Yellow[1] shaded with orange[3]
- **Horns:** Metallic copper[2]
- **Scales:** Splendid gold[2]
- **Ground:** Spice brown[1]

## GREEN DRAGON HEAD

- **Body:** Christmas green[1]
- **Breast plate:** Yellow[1] shaded with orange[3]
- **Ears:** Leaf green[1] shaded with linen[2]
- **Horns:** Splendid gold[2]
- **Background:** Autumn brown[1]

## DRAGON EGG

- **Shell:** Linen[2]
- **Hatchling:** Yellow[1] shaded with orange[3]
- **Background:** Spice brown[1]

## CASTLE BACKGROUND (INTERIOR, INSIDE OF DOORS)

- **Birds:** Black[1]
- **Sky:** Blue heaven[1]
- **All rocks:** Medium gray[2] shaded with black[1] and highlighted with white[1]

## CASTLE DOORS AND GRASS

- **Castle doors and hinge nails:** Spice brown[1]
- **Door hinges:** Black[1]
- **Grass:** Thicket[2]

1 Delta Ceramcoat
2 FolkArt
3 Apple Barrel
4 DecoArt

Blade-entry hole

**Carved Dragon Castle Puzzle Pieces, Puzzle Frame,
Back Woodburning Pattern (B)**

**Carved Dragon Castle Puzzle Castle Doors (Interior) (A)**

**Bottom Red Dragon**

**Carved Dragon Castle Puzzle Castle Doors (Exterior) (A)**

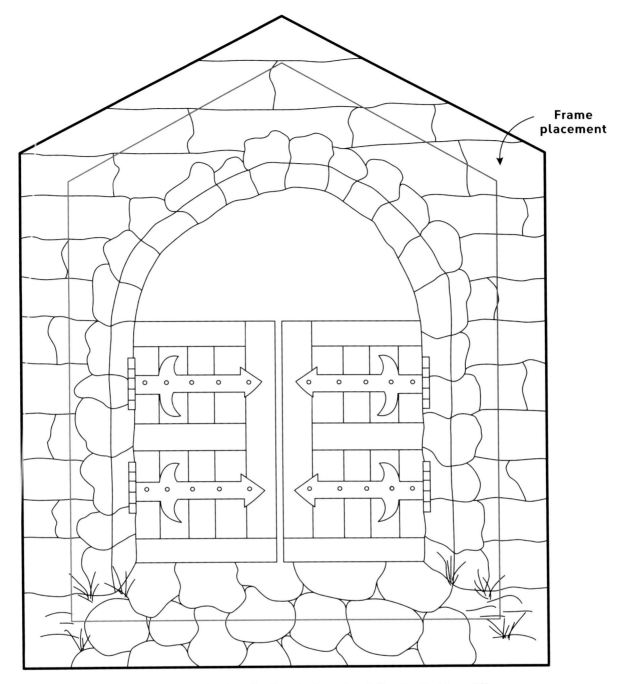

**Frame placement**

Carved Dragon Castle Puzzle Castle Interior / Castle Bottom (C)

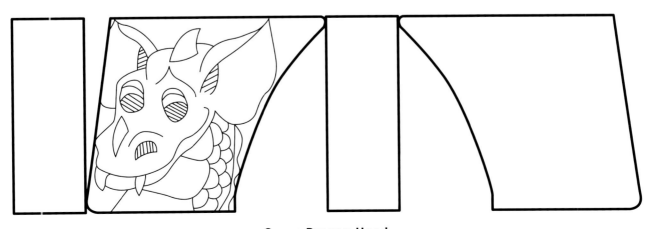

**Green Dragon Head**

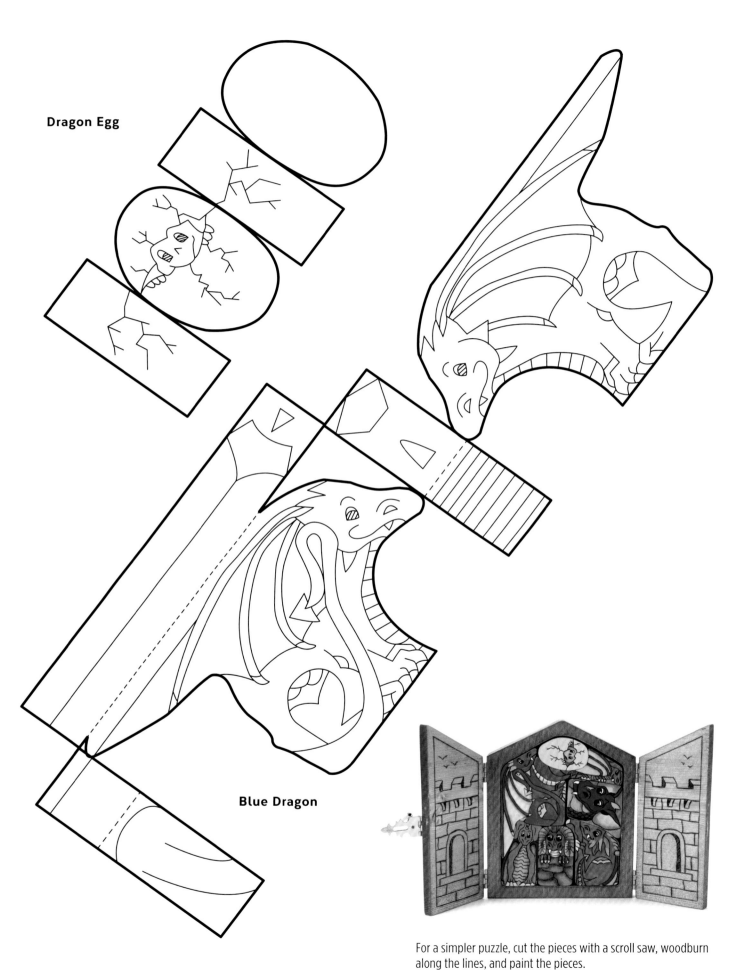

**Dragon Egg**

**Blue Dragon**

For a simpler puzzle, cut the pieces with a scroll saw, woodburn along the lines, and paint the pieces.

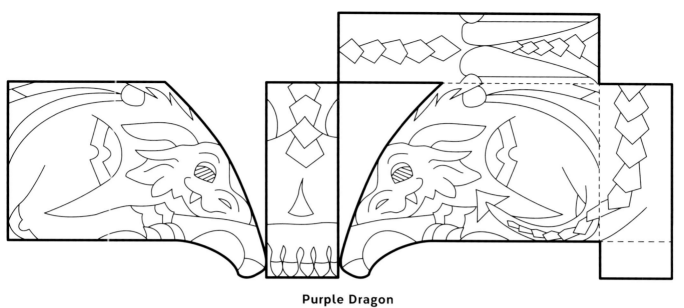

**Purple Dragon**

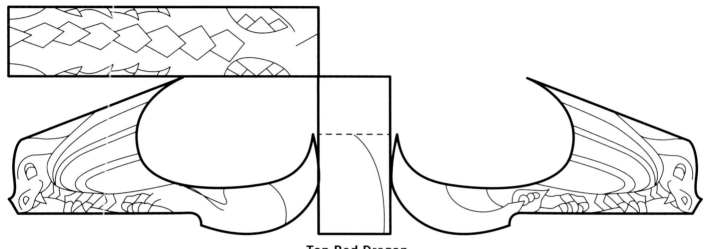

**Top Red Dragon**

**Full Green Dragon**

PROJECT:

# Once Upon a Time

I grew up with my mom reading fairy tales for bedtime stories. When I mentioned designing a "Prince and Princess" puzzle, I had orders before it was even designed. For Christmas, a friend had ordered two puzzles for her granddaughters. A week before Christmas, their house was broken into and all the packages under the tree opened. When they arrived back home, the only two packages taken from under the tree were the two Prince and Princess puzzles. We both laughed at thieves having such good taste. A rush order for two more puzzles was then in order.

## MATERIALS:

- Pine, ¼" (6mm) thick: front A, back C, 2 each 6" x 7" (152mm x 178mm)
- Pine, ¾" (19mm) thick: center B, 6" x 7" (152mm x 178mm)
- Acetone or graphite paper
- Wire brads: #19 by 1" (25mm)
- Brass hinges: 4 each ¾" x ¾" (19mm x 19mm)
- Brass-plated hasp: ¾" x 1⅞" (19mm x 48mm)
- Brass screws: 20 each #1 by ⅜" (10mm)
- Stain: Minwax special walnut 224
- Sandpaper: 120 grit
- Tape: clear double-sided
- Acrylic paint

### PRINCE
- **Jacket:** White[1]
- **Trousers:** Tuscan red[4]
- **Trouser stripes, shoulder brushes, jacket buttons, braid:** Metallic splendid gold[2]
- **Tops of shoulder brushes:** Metallic espresso[2]
- **Hair, shoes:** Black[1]
- **Hands, face:** Flesh[1]

### PRINCESS
- **Main gown, jewels:** Metallic blue sapphire[2]
- **Arms, sleeve gusset, gown inset:** Metallic blue pearl[2]
- **Tiara:** Gunmetal gray[2]
- **Hands, face:** Flesh[1]
- **Hair:** Yellow[1]
- **Gown trim:** Metallic splendid gold[2]
- **Gown pin:** Solid bronze[2]
- **Front ruffles:** White[1]

### KNIGHT
- **Body:** Gunmetal gray[2]
- **Shield trim, helmet plume, cross, lance ball:** Tuscan red[4]
- **Armor trim:** Solid bronze[2]
- **Helmet stripes:** Black[1]

### COACH
- **Body:** Metallic amethyst[2]
- **Tops, wheel insides, top of curtain:** Metallic plum[2]
- **Wheel rims, fringe:** Metallic splendid gold[2]
- **Ground:** Medium gray[2]

### DRAGON
- **Body:** Copenhagen blue[4]
- **Wings:** Oyster white[1], shaded with Copenhagen blue[4]
- **Scales:** Metallic copper[2]

### HORSE
- **Body:** Oyster white[1]
- **Mane, tail:** Bambi brown[1]
- **Tassels, blanket, swag trim:** Metallic blue topaz[2]
- **Blanket trim, neck swag:** Metallic splendid gold[2]
- **Swag trim:** Solid bronze[2]
- **Grass:** Thicket[2]

### FAIRY GODMOTHER
- **Gown:** Metallic Christmas green[2]
- **Gown trim, headdress:** Metallic peridot[2]
- **Star, headband, gown neck trim, shoes:** Metallic splendid gold[2]
- **Wand handle:** Metallic copper[2]

### FROG
- **Lily pad:** Thicket[2]
- **Water:** Blue heaven[1]
- **Crown top:** Metallic regal red[2]
- **Crown bottom:** Metallic splendid gold[2]
- **Crown jewels:** Metallic Christmas green[2]
- **Body:** Leaf green[1]
- **Spots:** Bright yellow[3]
- **Chest:** Oyster white[1] mixed with bright yellow[3]

### CROWN
- **Top:** Metallic regal red[2]
- **Bottom:** Metallic splendid gold[2]
- **Jewels:** Metallic Christmas green[2], metallic bright red[2]

---

1 Delta Ceramcoat
2 FolkArt
3 Apple Barrel
4 DecoArt

Blade-entry
hole

**Once Upon a Time Puzzle Pieces,
Puzzle Frame, Back Woodburning Pattern (B)**

**Once Upon a Time Puzzle Castle Doors (Interior) (A)**

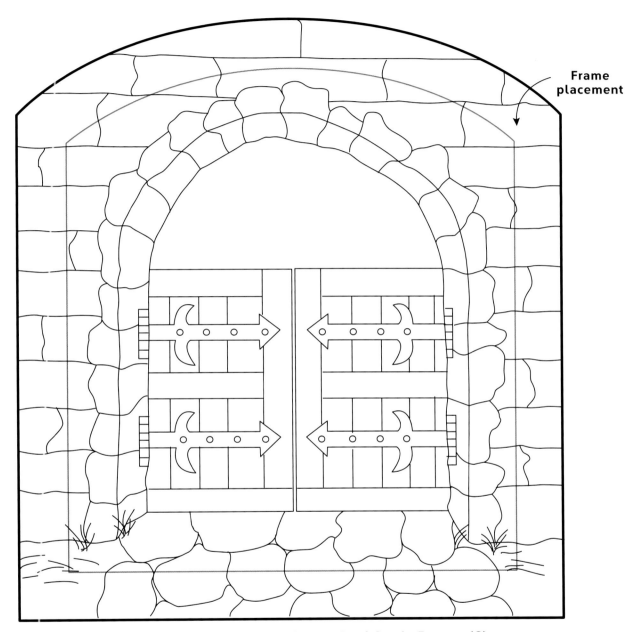

**Frame placement**

**Once Upon a Time Puzzle Castle Interior / Castle Bottom (C)**

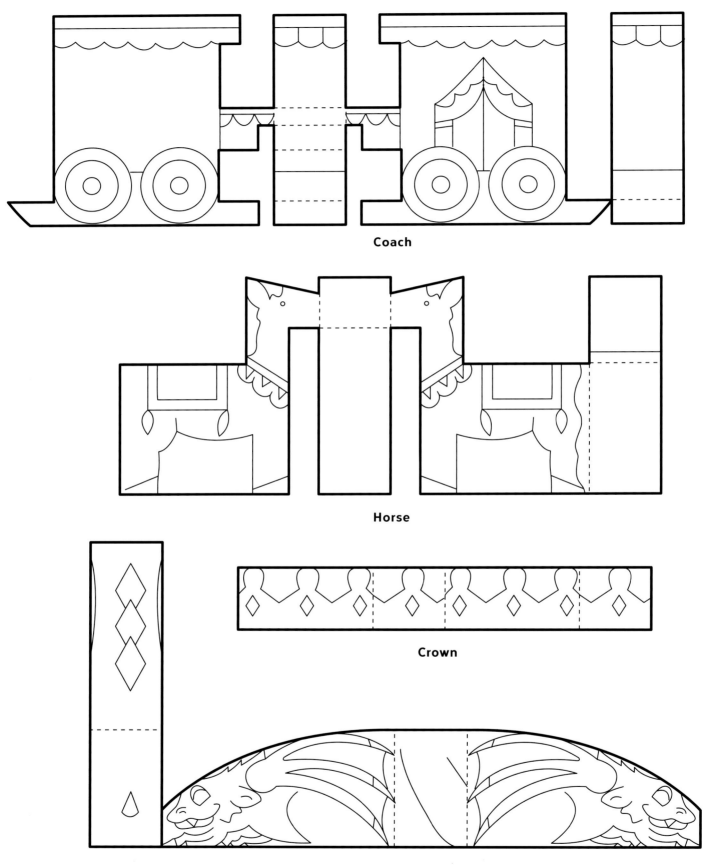

**Coach**

**Horse**

**Crown**

**Dragon**

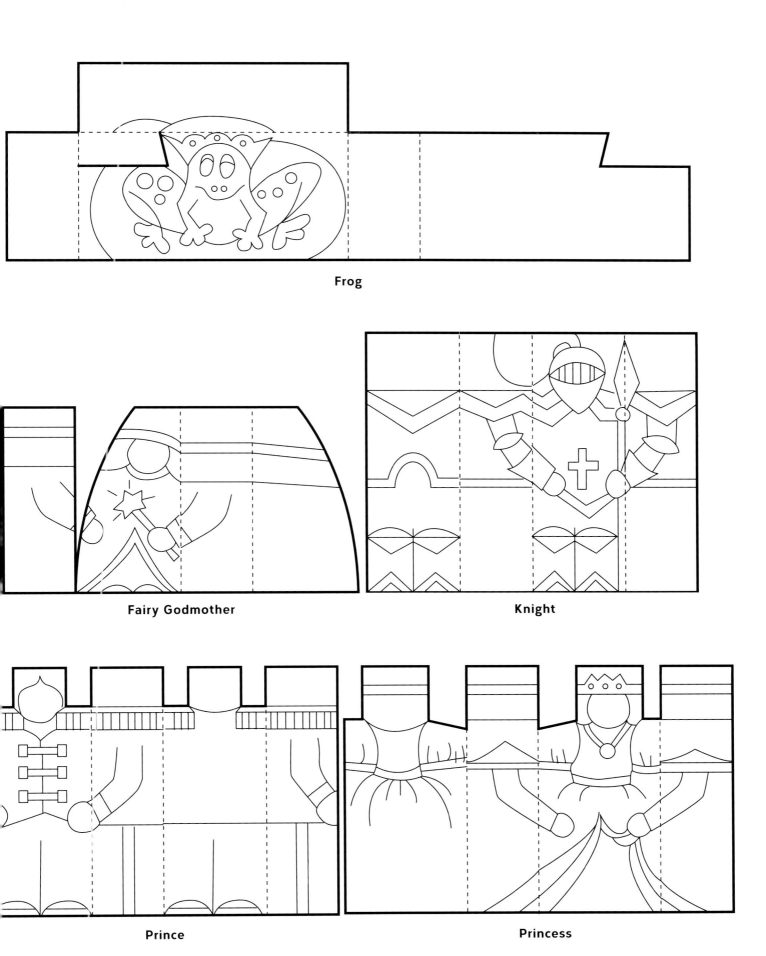

Frog

Fairy Godmother

Knight

Prince

Princess

PROJECT:

# Noah's Ark Two Ways

The Noah's Ark puzzle needed to be "two by two," and it took a bit of thinking to make that happen. A nephew saw the first ark puzzle prototype. He wanted one for his children, but asked if I could make it look more like an actual ark. So, the more popular ark shape/ramp came into being. I have included both versions here. After cutting the animals, slice them in half through the thickness to create a pair. Remember there are often separate woodburning and painting patterns for the male and female of each animal.

## MATERIALS

### OPTION 1 (STANDARD PUZZLE BOX)

- Pine, ¼" (6mm) thick: front A, back C, 2 each 6" x 7" (152mm x 178mm)
- Pine, ¾" (19mm) thick: center B, 6" x 7" (152mm x 178mm)
- Brass hinges: 4 each ¾" x ¾" (19mm x 19mm)

### OPTION 2 (ARK-STYLE BOX)

- Pine, ¼" (6mm) thick: front A, back C, 2 each 6" x 7" (152mm x 178mm)
- Basswood, 1" (25mm) thick: center B, 6" x 7" (152mm x 178mm)
- Basswood, ¾" (19mm) thick: bow and stern (D), 4½" x 12" (114mm x 305mm)
- Acetone or graphite paper
- Wire brads: #19 by 1" (25mm)
- Brass-plated hasp: ¾" x 1⅞" (19mm x 48mm)
- Brass screws: 20 each #1 by ⅜" (10mm)
- Brass hinges: 2 each ¾" x ¾" (19mm x 19mm)
- Stain: Minwax special walnut 224
- Sandpaper: 120 grit
- Tape: clear double-sided
- Acrylic paint

### NOAH
- **Robe:** Dark brown[1]
- **Headdress:** Linen[2]
- **Staff, headband:** Burnt umber[1]
- **Beard, dove:** White[1]
- **Leaf:** Christmas green[1]
- **Face, hands:** Flesh[1]

### MRS. NOAH
- **Robe:** Aspen green[2]
- **Headdress:** Sage[2]
- **Pot:** Burnt sienna[1]
- **Grain:** Raw sienna[1]
- **Face, hands:** Flesh[1]

### ELEPHANTS
- **Body:** Bridgeport gray[1]
- **Tusks:** White[1]

### GIRAFFES
- **Body:** Golden brown[1]
- **Spots, horns:** Spice brown[1]

### LION
- **Body:** Camel[2]
- **Mane, tail tip:** Sierra brown[1]
- **Nose:** Spice brown[1]

### LIONESS
- **All:** Camel[2]
- **Nose:** Spice brown[1]

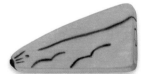

### RABBITS
- **All:** Bambi brown[1]

### HORSE #1
- **Body:** Spice brown[1]
- **Mane, tail:** Bambi brown[1]

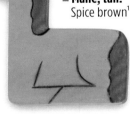

### HORSE #2
- **Body:** Bambi brown[1]
- **Mane, tail:** Spice brown[1]

### WHALES
- **Body:** Hippo grey[1]
- **Water:** Laguna blue[1]

### GEESE
- **Body:** White[1]
- **Bill:** Bright yellow[3]

### TURTLES
- **Body:** Old ivy[2]
- **Shell trim, spots:** Bambi brown[1]
- **Eyes:** White[1], black[1], with a white[1] highlight

### BEARS
- **All:** Brown velvet[1]

---

1 Delta Ceramcoat
2 FolkArt
3 Apple Barrel
4 DecoArt

**Noah's Ark Puzzle Pieces, Puzzle Frame,
Back Woodburning Pattern (Option 1 & 2) (B)**

**Blade-entry
hole**

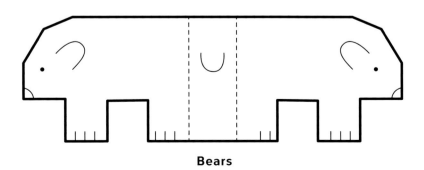

**Bears**

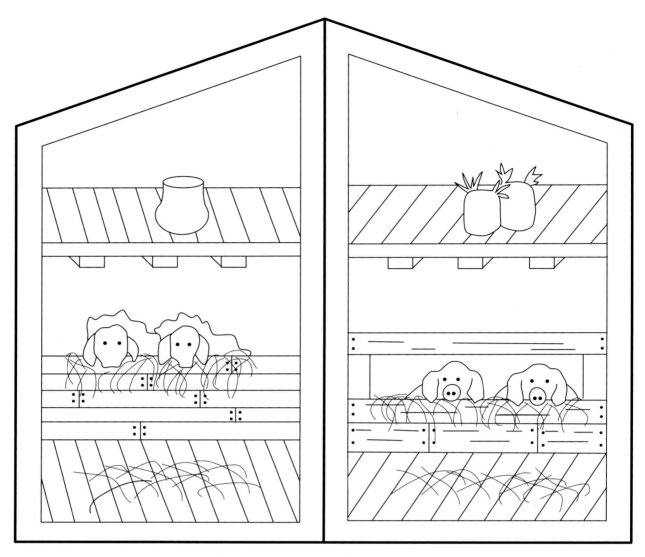

**Noah's Ark Puzzle Ark Doors (Interior Option 1) (A)**

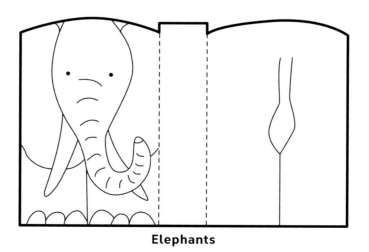

**Elephants**

**Cut on dashed line to separate doors
for Option 1 only**

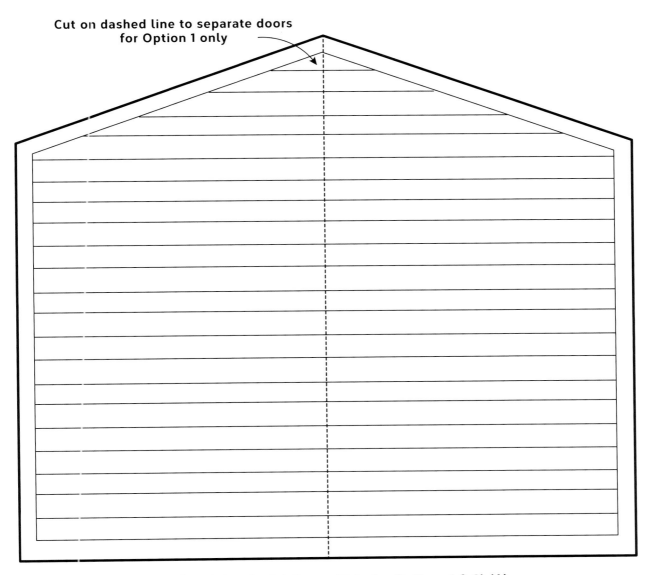

**Noah's Ark Puzzle Ark Doors (Exterior Options 1 & 2) (A)**

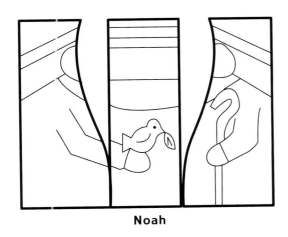

**Noah**

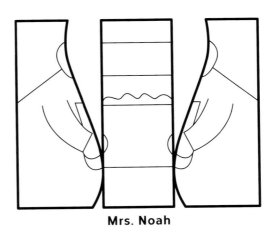

**Mrs. Noah**

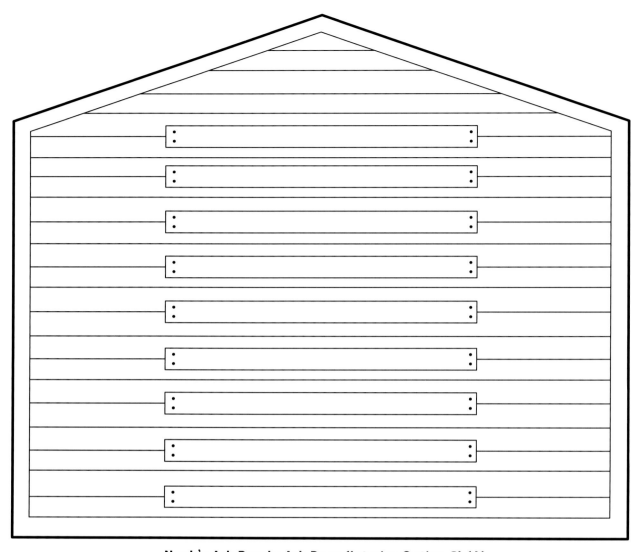

**Noah's Ark Puzzle Ark Door (Interior Option 2) (A)**

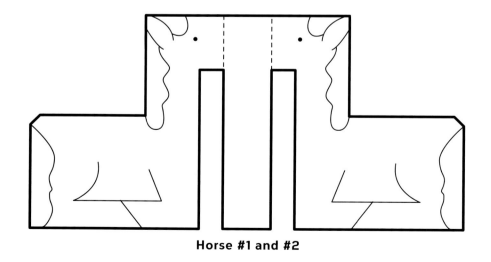

**Horse #1 and #2**

**Frame placement**

Noah's Ark Puzzle Ark Interior / Ark Bottom (Options 1 & 2) (C)

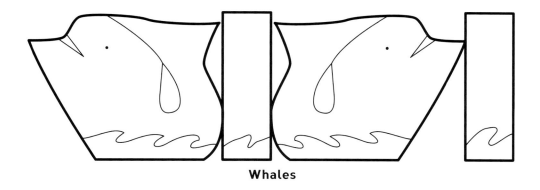

**Whales**

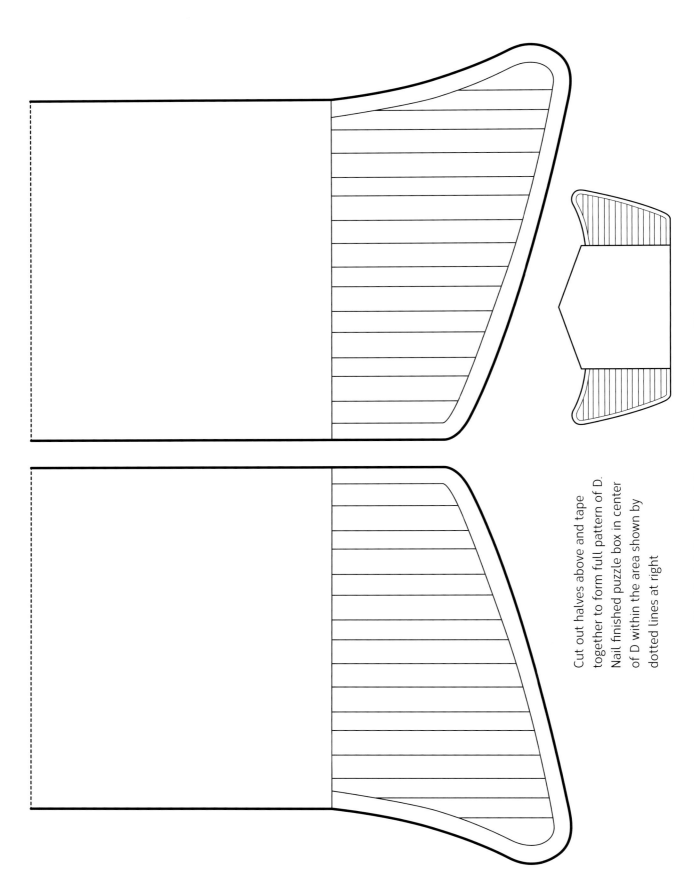

Cut out halves above and tape together to form full pattern of D. Nail finished puzzle box in center of D within the area shown by dotted lines at right

**Noah's Ark Puzzle Ark Bow and Stern Patterns (D)**

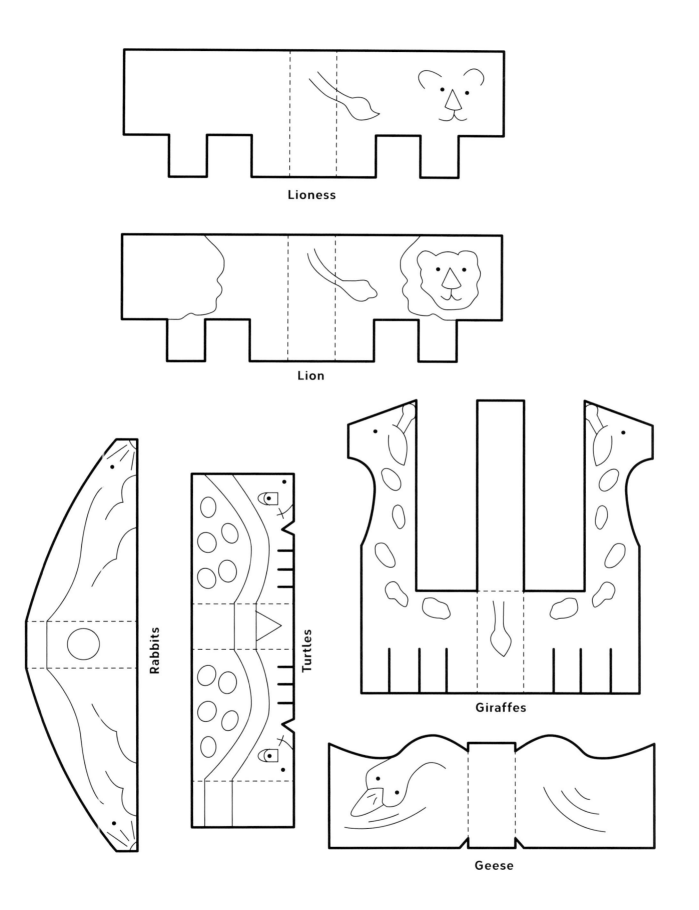

Lioness

Lion

Rabbits

Turtles

Giraffes

Geese

PROJECT:

# Jurassic Puzzle

The Jurassic (dinosaur) Puzzle was made for the once-small boy, Kevin. When he was about three, he lived and breathed dinosaurs. Before he discovered crayons or pencils, he would cut out dinosaur body parts from construction paper. He then used tape to assemble the bodies. I should have had stock in a clear-tape company. I put the names of the dinosaurs on the puzzle solution for parents. The children can already name all of the dinosaurs.

## MATERIALS:

- Pine, ¼" (6mm) thick: front A, back C, 2 each 6" x 7" (152mm x 178mm)
- Pine, ¾" (19mm) thick: center B, 6" x 7" (152mm x 178mm)
- Acetone or graphite paper
- Wire brads: #19 by 1" (25mm)
- Brass hinges: 4 each ¾" x ¾" (19mm x 19mm)
- Brass-plated hasp: ¾" x 1⅞" (19mm x 48mm)
- Brass screws: 20 each #1 by ⅜" (10mm)
- Stain: Minwax special walnut 224
- Sandpaper: 120 grit
- Tape: clear double-sided
- Acrylic paint

### BRONTOSAURUS
- **Body:** Bridgeport grey[1] shaded with medium gray[2] and black[1]
- **Water:** Laguna blue[1]
- **Sky:** Blue heaven[1]

### STEGOSAURUS
- **Body:** Aspen[2]
- **Chest:** Sage[2]
- **Claws, tail:** Dark brown[1]
- **Fins:** Aspen[2] shaded with dark brown[1]
- **Ground:** Cinnamon[2]
- **Sky:** Blue heaven[1]

### PTERADON
- **Wings:** Wet wings with water, then paint and shade with medium gray[2] and tapestry wine[3]
- **Back, body, head:** Tapestry wine[3]
- **Breast:** Bambi brown[1] with tapestry wine[3]
- **Feet, bill:** Dark brown[1]
- **Claws, eyes:** Black[1]

### STYRACOSAURUS
- **Body:** Burnt sienna[1]
- **Head:** Cinnamon[2]
- **Horns:** Dark brown[1]
- **Chest:** Ivory[1] shaded with burnt sienna[1]
- **Grass:** Thicket[2]

### DIMETRODON
- **Body:** Nutmeg[3]
- **Fins:** Ivory[1] shaded with nutmeg[3]
- **Claws:** Black[1]
- **Veins:** Burnt umber[1]

### TYRANNOSAURUS REX
- **Body:** Royal violet[3]
- **Chest:** Ivory[1] shaded with royal violet[3]
- **Grass:** Thicket[2]

- - - - - - - - - - - - - - -

1 Delta Ceramcoat
2 FolkArt
3 Apple Barrel
4 DecoArt

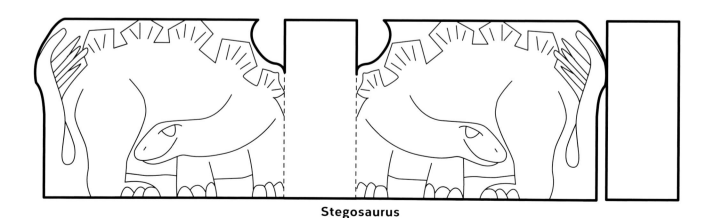

**Stegosaurus**

**Blade-entry hole**

**Jurassic Puzzle Pieces, Puzzle Frame (B)**

**Jurassic Puzzle Doors (Interior) (A)**

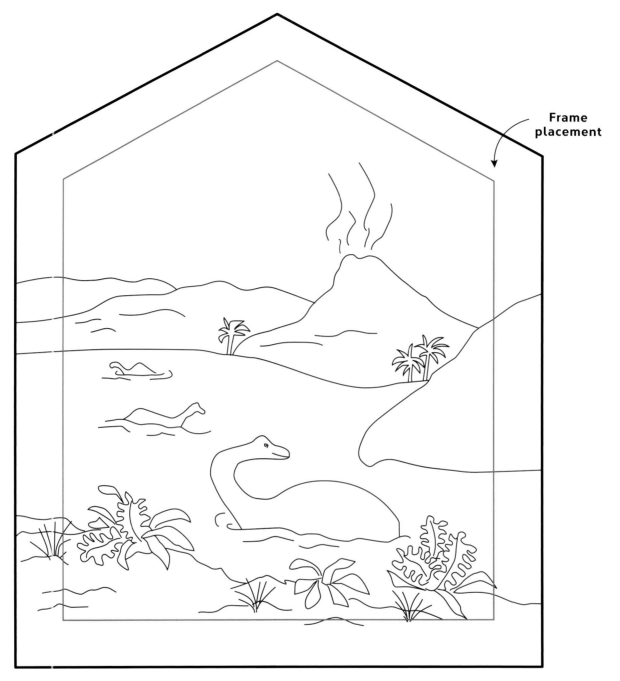

**Frame placement**

**Jurassic Puzzle Box Interior / Box Bottom (C)**

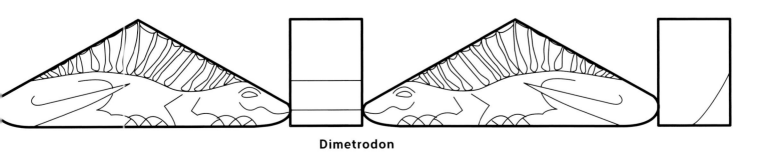

**Dimetrodon**

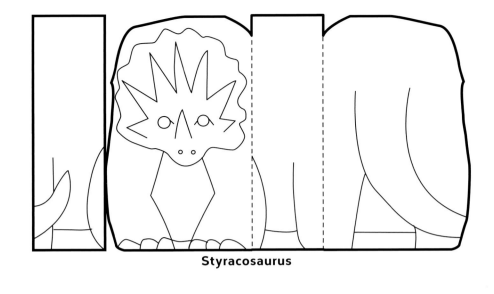

**Styracosaurus**

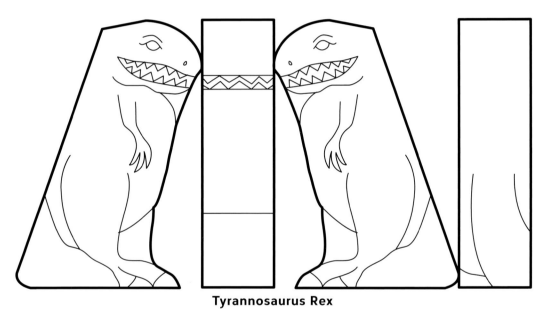

**Tyrannosaurus Rex**

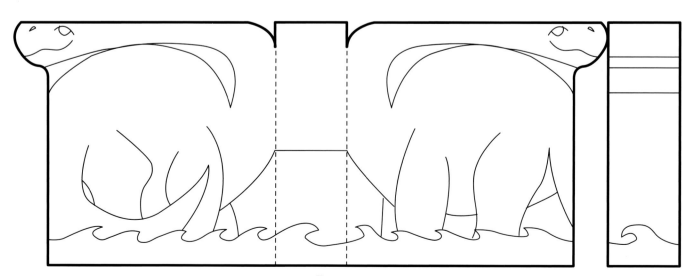

**Brontosaurus**

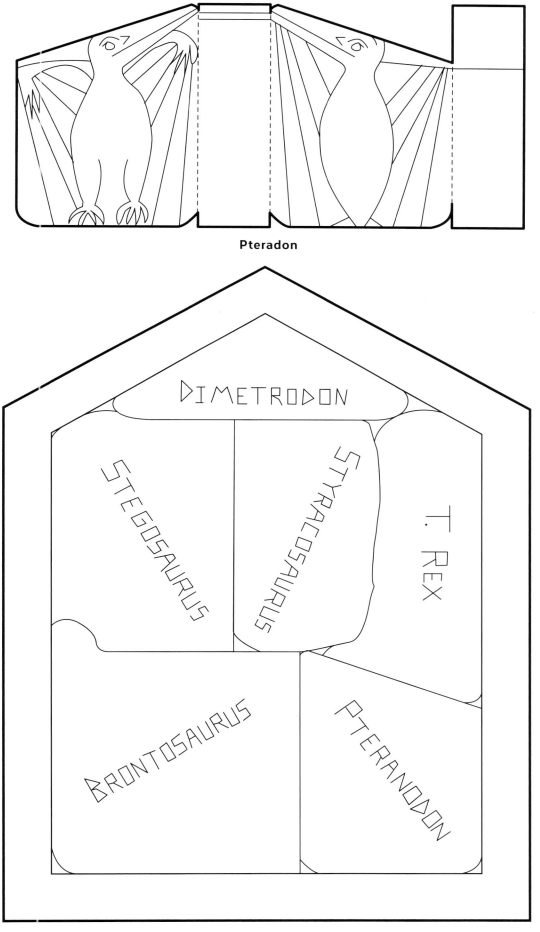

**Pteradon**

**Jurassic Puzzle Box Back Woodburning Pattern (C)**

PROJECT:

# Merry Christmas

Christmas is my favorite time of year, so it didn't take me long to come up with a list of Christmas items for a puzzle. But, choosing the ones to include, sizing them properly, and arranging them to fit into my standard puzzle box took a bit longer.

## MATERIALS:

- Pine, ¼" (6mm) thick: front A, back C, 2 each 6" x 7" (152mm x 178mm)
- Basswood, ¾" (19mm) thick: center B, 6" x 7" (152mm x 178mm)
- Acetone or graphite paper
- Wire brads: #19 by 1" (25mm)
- Brass hinges: 4 each ¾" x ¾" (19mm x 19mm)
- Brass-plated hasp: ¾" x 1⅞" (19mm x 48mm)
- Brass screws: 20 each #1 by ⅜" (10mm)
- Stain: Minwax special walnut 224
- Sandpaper: 120 grit
- Tape: clear double-sided
- Acrylic paint

### SANTA
- **Suit:** Tompte red[1]
- **Trim, beard:** White[1]
- **Shoes, gloves:** Black[1]
- **Candy cane:** Tompte red[1], white[1]
- **Face:** Flesh[1]

### SNOWMAN
- **Body:** White[1]
- **Nose:** Orange[3]
- **Scarf, hat:** Navy blue[1]
- **Hat trim, gloves:** Tompte red[1]
- **Broom:** Raw sienna[1]
- **Broom handle:** Burnt sienna[1]
- **Sign:** Spice brown[1]

### CHRISTMAS TREE
- **Tree:** Christmas green[1]
- **Trunk:** Burnt umber[1]
- **Tinsel:** Splendid gold[2]
- **Ornaments:** Metallic blue[2], metallic topaz[2], metallic rose[2], metallic peridot[2], metallic amethyst[2], metallic red[2]

### BELLS
- **All:** Metallic silver[2]
- **Ribbon:** Christmas green[1]
- **Clappers:** Metallic pewter gray[2]

### SLEIGH
- **Body:** Tompte red[1]
- **Runners:** Metallic silver[2]
- **Trim:** Splendid gold[2]

### STOCKING
- **Body:** Navy blue[1]
- **Trim:** White[1]
- **Bear:** Brown velvet[1]

### NATIVITY
- **Stable outside:** Spice brown[1]
- **Stable inside:** Brown velvet[1]
- **Joseph robe:** Burnt sienna[1]
- **Joseph headdress:** Goose feather[2]
- **Joseph staff, headdress band:** Burnt umber[1]
- **Joseph face, hands:** Flesh[1]
- **Mary robe:** Copen blue[1]
- **Mary headdress:** Blue haven[1]
- **Mary face, hands:** Flesh[1]
- **Cradle:** Burnt sienna[1]
- **Blanket:** Goose feather[2]
- **Jesus face:** Flesh[1]
- **Star:** Splendid gold[2]

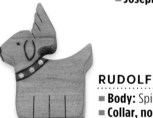

### RUDOLF
- **Body:** Spice brown[1]
- **Collar, nose:** Tompte red[1]

### SANTA
- **Hat:** Tompte red[1]
- **Trim, beard:** White[1]
- **Face:** Flesh[1]

1 Delta Ceramcoat
2 FolkArt
3 Apple Barrel
4 DecoArt

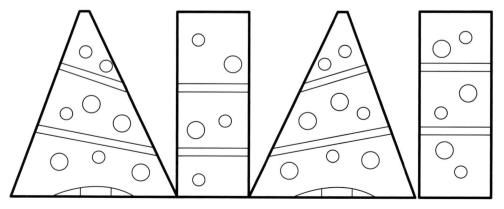

**Christmas Tree**

**Blade-entry hole**

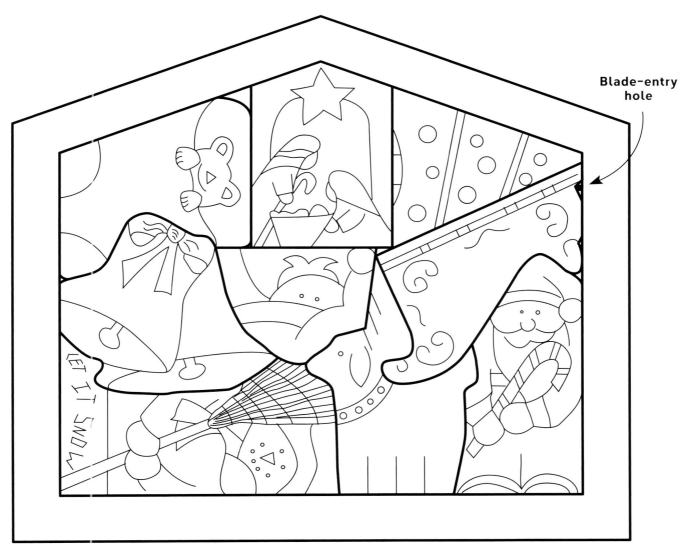

**Merry Christmas Puzzle Pieces, Puzzle Frame,
Back Woodburning Pattern (B)**

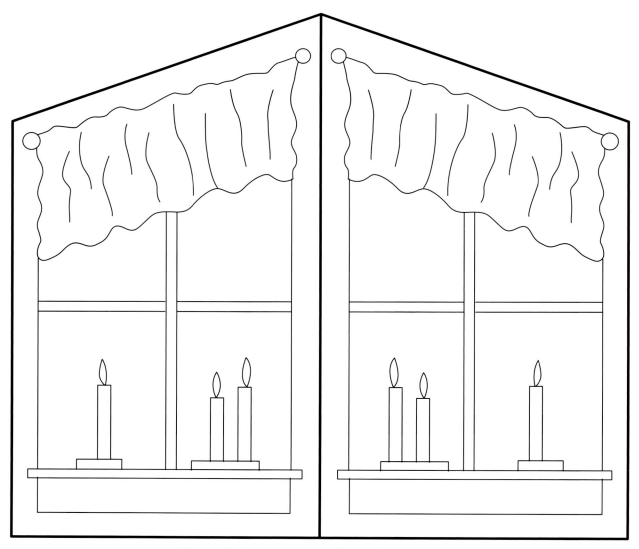

**Merry Christmas Puzzle Doors (Interior) (A)**

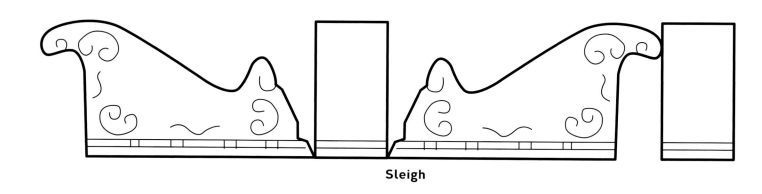

**Sleigh**

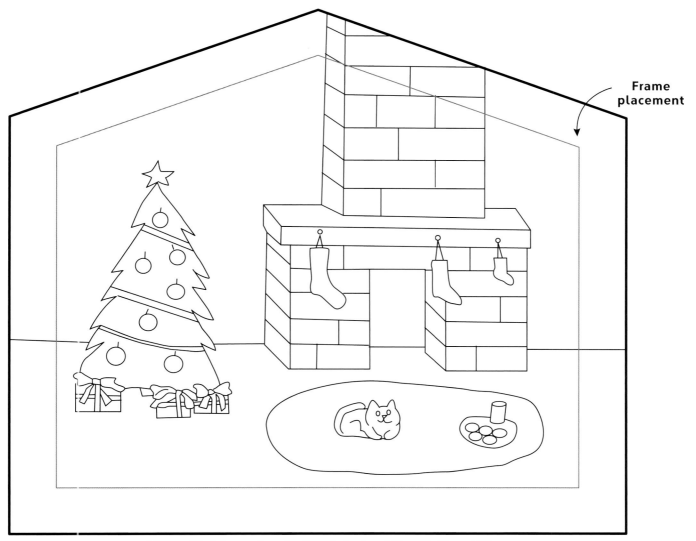

**Frame placement**

**Merry Christmas Puzzle Box Interior / Box Bottom (C)**

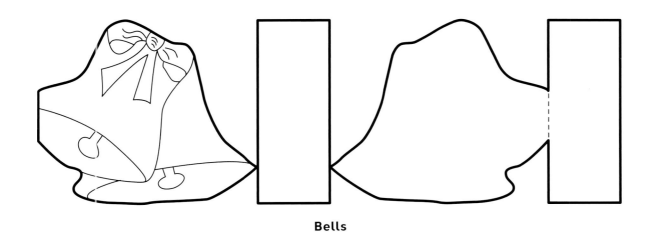

**Bells**

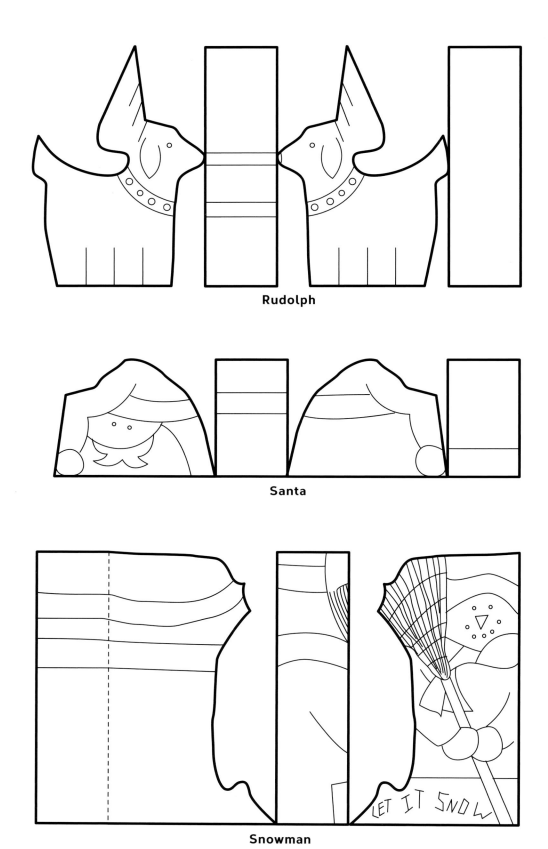

Rudolph

Santa

Snowman

LET IT SNOW

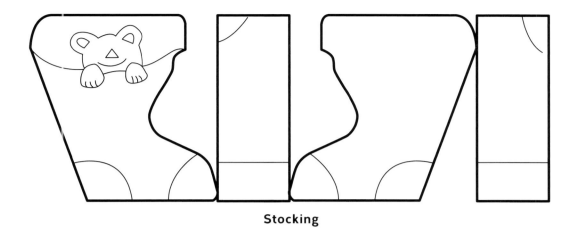

**Stocking**

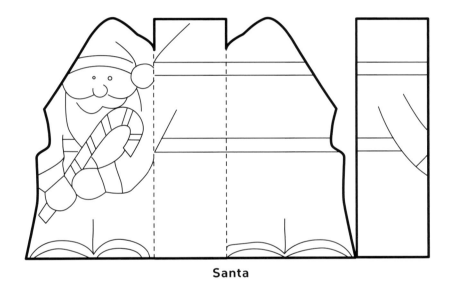

**Santa**

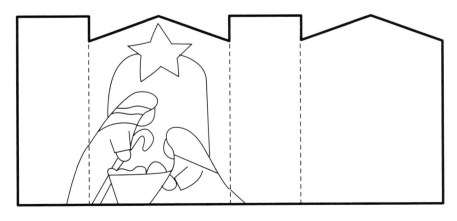

**Nativity**

PROJECT:

# Squished Santas

Christmas is the one time of year I truly enjoy. I love anything relating to Santa Claus. I have carved Santa figures and faces on and out of anything wooden. Spoons, rolling pins, darning eggs, thread spools, and more items than I can think of right now. I think I can turn most anything into a Santa Claus, which made this Squished Santa puzzle easy to design.

**MATERIALS:**

- Pine, ¼" (6mm) thick: front A, back C, 2 each 6" x 7" (152mm x 178mm)
- Basswood, ¾" (19mm) thick: center B, 6" x 7" (152mm x 178mm)
- Acetone or graphite paper
- Wire brads: #19 by 1" (25mm)
- Brass hinges: 4 each ¾" x ¾" (19mm x 19mm)
- Brass-plated hasp: ¾" x 1⅞" (19mm x 48mm)
- Brass screws: 20 each #1 by ⅜" (10mm)
- Stain: Minwax special walnut 224
- Sandpaper: 120 grit
- Tape: clear double-sided
- Acrylic paint

### ALL SANTAS

- **Suits:** Tompte red[1]
- **Suit trim, beards, hair:** White[1]
- **Gloves, boots:** Black[1]
- **Bags:** Christmas green[1]
- **Buckles:** Gold[2]

1 Delta Ceramcoat
2 FolkArt
3 Apple Barrel
4 DecoArt

## SQUISHED SANTAS: Patterns

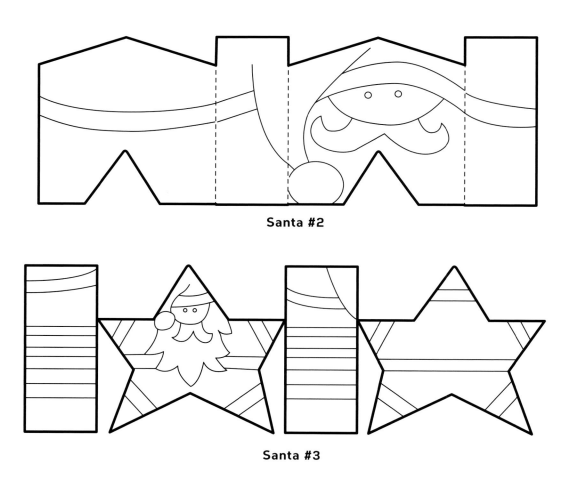

Santa #2

Santa #3

**Squished Santas Puzzle Pieces, Puzzle Frame,
Back Woodburning Pattern (B)**

Blade-entry
hole

**Santa #7**

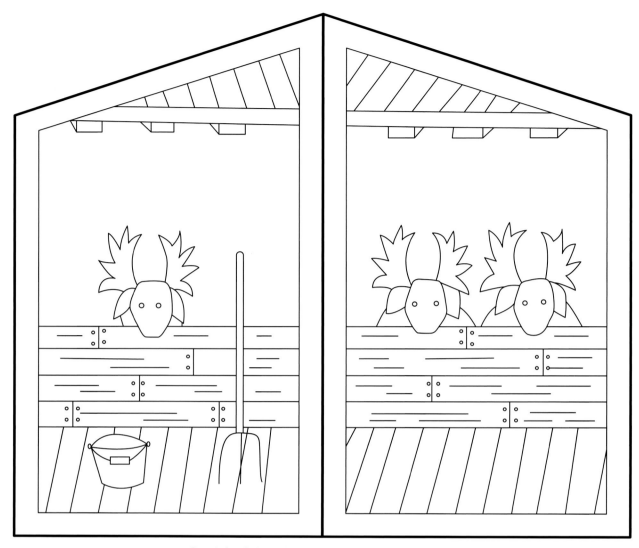

**Squished Santas Puzzle Doors (Interior) (A)**

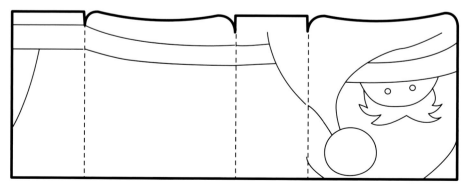

**Santa #8**

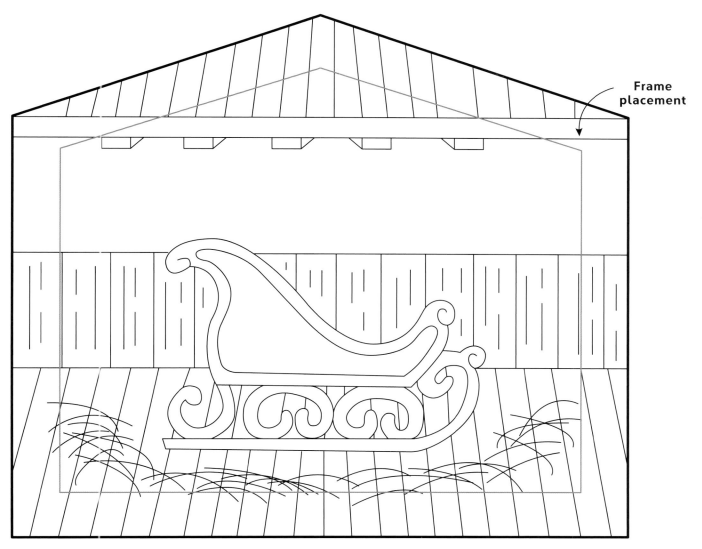

**Frame placement**

**Squished Santas Puzzle Barn Interior / Barn Bottom (C)**

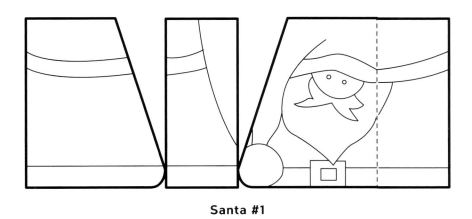

**Santa #1**

For a different look, transfer this alternative pattern
for the Squished Santas Puzzle Barn Interior (C) to the
blank and carve and paint or woodburn the design.

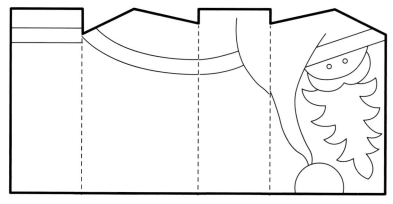

Santa #9

**Frame placement**

**Squished Santas Puzzle Alternative Barn Interior / Barn Bottom (C)**

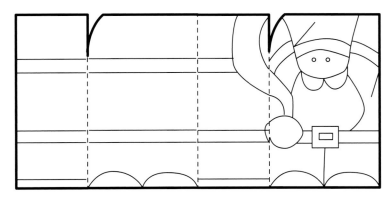

**Santa #6**

**Squished Santas Puzzle Doors (Exterior) (A)**

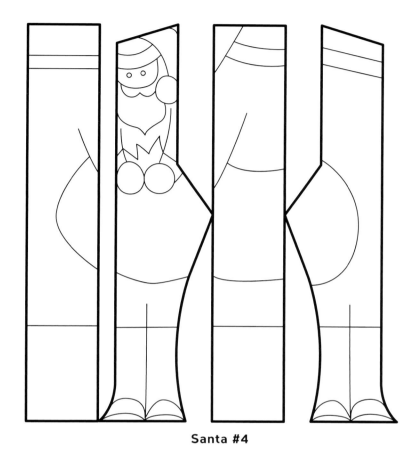

**Santa #4**

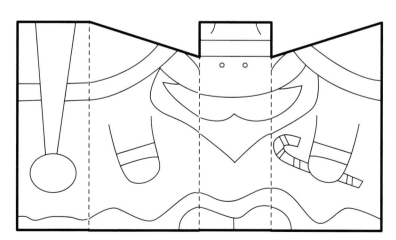

**Santa #5**

# O Holy Night Nativity

This is the puzzle that started it all. A friend asked me to make a few puzzles for her children based on an old nativity set; she wanted to give one to each of them for Christmas. After some thought, I designed a smaller nativity puzzle with detailed pieces and added a background stable scene and stable doors.

## MATERIALS

- Pine, ¼" (6mm) thick: front A, back C, 2 each 6" x 7" (152mm x 178mm)
- Pine, ¾" (19mm) thick: center B, 6" x 7" (152mm x 178mm)
- Acetone or graphite paper
- Wire brads: #19 by 1" (25mm)
- Brass hinges: 4 each ¾" x ¾" (19mm x 19mm)
- Brass-plated hasp: ¾" x 1⅞" (19mm x 48mm)
- Brass screws: 20 each #1 by ⅜" (10mm)
- Stain: Minwax special walnut 224
- Sandpaper: 120 grit
- Tape: clear double-sided
- Acrylic paint

## STAR
- **All:** Splendid gold[2]

### KING #1
- **Robe:** Metallic Christmas green[2]
- **Headdress:** Metallic peridot[2]
- **Chest:** Metallic gunmetal[2] with metallic gold[2] clasp
- **Face, hands:** Flesh[1] tinted with burnt umber[1]
- **Crown:** Splendid gold[2]

### KNEELING SHEPHERD
- **Robe:** Burnt sienna[1]
- **Headdress:** Linen[2]
- **Headband, staff:** Burnt umber[1]
- **Face, hands:** Flesh[1]

### KING #2
- **Robe:** Metallic amethyst[2]
- **Headdress:** Metallic plum[2]
- **Chest:** Metallic Sahara gold[2] with metallic gunmetal[2] clasp
- **Face, hands:** Flesh[1]
- **Crown:** Splendid gold[2]

### KING #3
- **Robe:** Metallic sapphire[2]
- **Headdress:** Metallic blue pearl[2]
- **Bottle:** Metallic solid bronze[2]
- **Cork:** Mushroom[2]
- **Face, hands:** Flesh[1]
- **Crown:** Splendid gold[2]

### STANDING SHEPHERD
- **Robe:** Georgia clay[1]
- **Headdress:** Sandstone[2]
- **Headband, staff:** Burnt umber[1]
- **Face, hands:** Flesh[1]

### MARY
- **Robe:** Copen blue[1]
- **Headdress:** Blue heaven[1]
- **Face, hands:** Flesh[1]

### BABY JESUS
- **Cradle:** Spice brown[1]
- **Bedding:** Goose feather[3]
- **Face:** Flesh[1]

### JOSEPH
- **Robe:** Coffee bean[2]
- **Headdress:** Mushroom[2]
- **Headband, staff:** Burnt umber[1]
- **Face, hands:** Flesh[1]

## ANGEL
- **Robe:** Metallic rose[2]
- **Wings:** Metallic pearl white[2]
- **Face, hands:** Flesh[1]
- **Halo, robe trim:** Splendid gold[2]

### DONKEY
- **All:** Medium gray[2]

### SHEEP
- **All:** Wicker white[2]

### CAMEL
- **Body:** Spice brown[1]
- **Blanket:** Blue topaz[2]
- **Blanket trim:** Inca gold[2]

### COW
- **All:** Raw sienna[1]

---

1 Delta Ceramcoat
2 FolkArt
3 Apple Barrel
4 DecoArt

**Blade-entry hole**

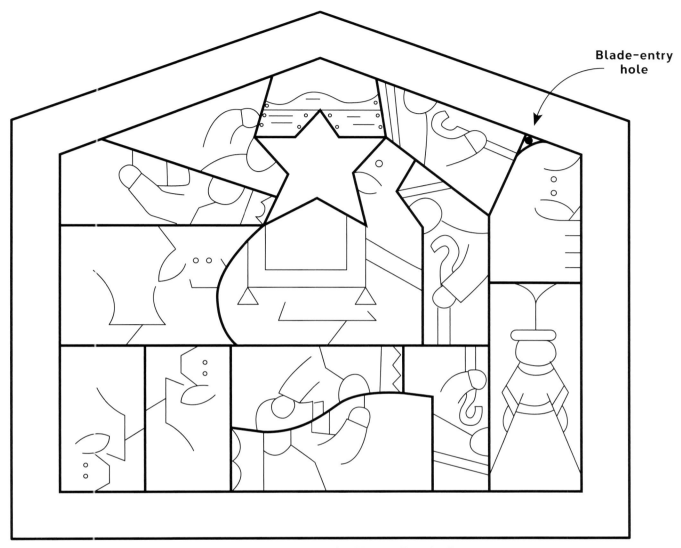

O Holy Night Nativity Puzzle Pieces, Puzzle Frame,
Back Woodburning Pattern (B)

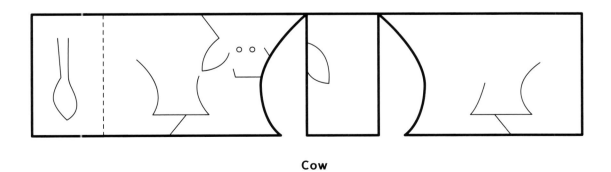

Cow

**O Holy Night Nativity Puzzle Stable Doors (Interior) (A)**

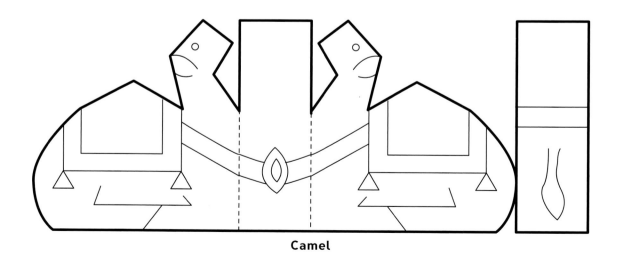

**Camel**

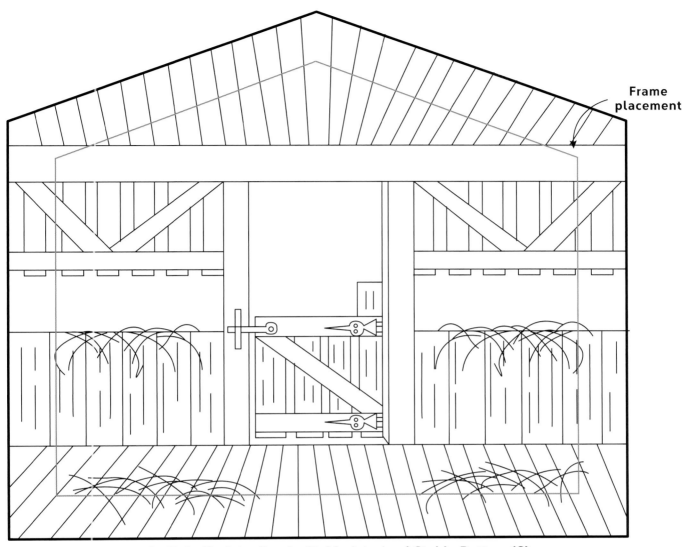

Frame placement

**O Holy Night Nativity Puzzle Stable Interior / Stable Bottom (C)**

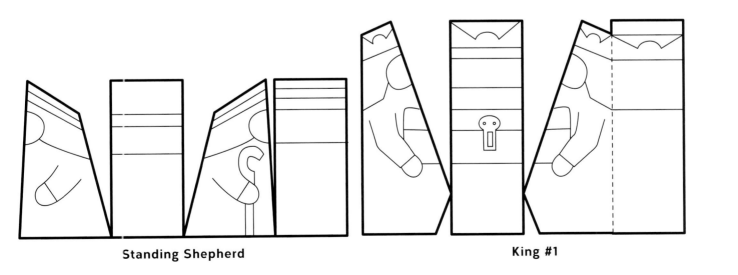

**Standing Shepherd**

**King #1**

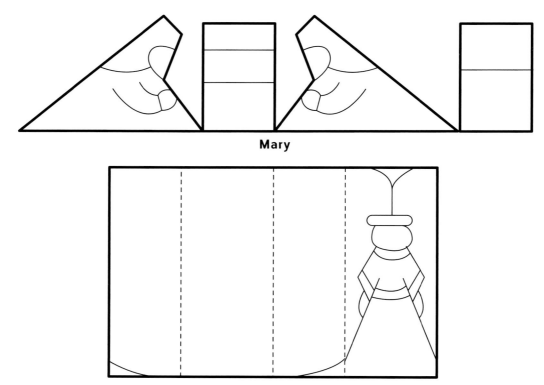

**Mary**

**Angel**

**Kneeling Shepherd**

**Baby Jesus**

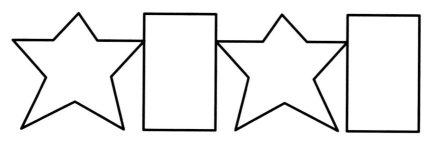

**Star**

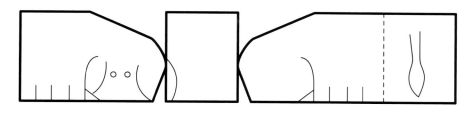

**Donkey**

**Sheep (make 2)**

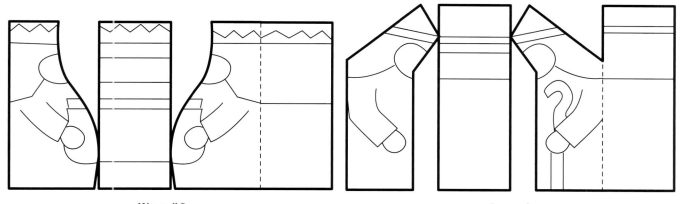

**King #2**

**Joseph**

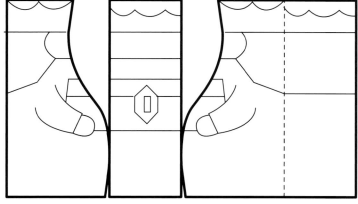

**King #3**

PROJECT:

# A Heap of Snowmen

Snowmen always bring a smile to my face. They remind me of childhood days, sledding parties, building snowmen, snowball fights at our one-room country school, and, being a dairy farmer's daughter, drinking lots of hot chocolate. When my son was small, we also spent many a day sledding down our pond dike, building snowmen, and eating "snow" ice cream. A snowman puzzle was just waiting to be created.

**MATERIALS:**

- Pine, ¼" (6mm) thick: front A, back C, 2 each 6" x 7" (152mm x 178mm)
- Pine, ¾" (19mm) thick: center B, 6" x 7" (152mm x 178mm)
- Acetone or graphite paper
- Wire brads: #19 by 1" (25mm)
- Brass hinges: 4 each ¾" x ¾" (19mm x 19mm)
- Brass-plated hasp: ¾" x 1⅞" (19mm x 48mm)
- Brass screws: 20 each #1 by ⅜" (10mm)
- Stain: Minwax special walnut 224
- Sandpaper: 120 grit
- Tape: clear double-sided
- Acrylic paint

### ALL SNOWMEN
- **Bodies:** White[1]
- **Carrot noses:** Orange[3]

### SNOWMAN WITH BROOM
- **Broom:** Gilded oak[2]
- **Broom handle:** Burnt umber[1]
- **Hat, muffler stripes, shawl:** Neon pink[3]
- **Earmuffs, hat fringe:** Medium gray[2]

### SKIER SNOWMAN
- **Pants:** Christmas green[1]
- **Jacket, pants patch:** Leaf green[1]
- **Scarf trim:** Yellow[1]
- **Skis:** Burnt umber[1]
- **Buttons:** Splendid gold[2]
- **Gloves, boots:** Black[1]

### BIRDHOUSE SNOWMAN
- **Coat:** Navy blue[1]
- **Bird, birdhouse, scarf:** Tompte red[1]
- **Hat trim:** Christmas green[1]
- **Bird house roof:** Spice brown[1]
- **Hat, gloves, birdhouse hole:** Black[1]

### S'MORES SNOWMAN
- **Jacket:** Navy blue[1]
- **Tie:** Christmas green[1]
- **Candle, hat trim:** Tompte red[1]
- **Candle base, stick:** Burnt umber[1]
- **Candle flame:** Yellow[1]
- **Boots, gloves, hat:** Black[1]
- **Bucket:** Metallic aluminum[2]

### LET IT SNOW SNOWMAN
- **Hat, scarf:** Mallard green[1], white[1]
- **Sign:** Spice brown[1]

### SNOWBALLS SNOWMAN
- **Scarf, gloves, hat:** Tompte red[1]
- **Box inside:** Burnt umber[1]
- **Box outside:** Spice brown[1]

### HEART SNOWMAN
- **Hat, gloves:** Purple[1]
- **Scarf:** Lavender[2]
- **Heart, hat trim, holly trim:** Tompte red[1]
- **Holly:** Christmas green[1]

1 Delta Ceramcoat
2 FolkArt
3 Apple Barrel
4 DecoArt

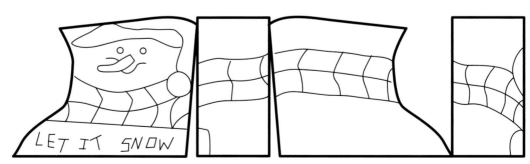

**Let It Snow Snowman**

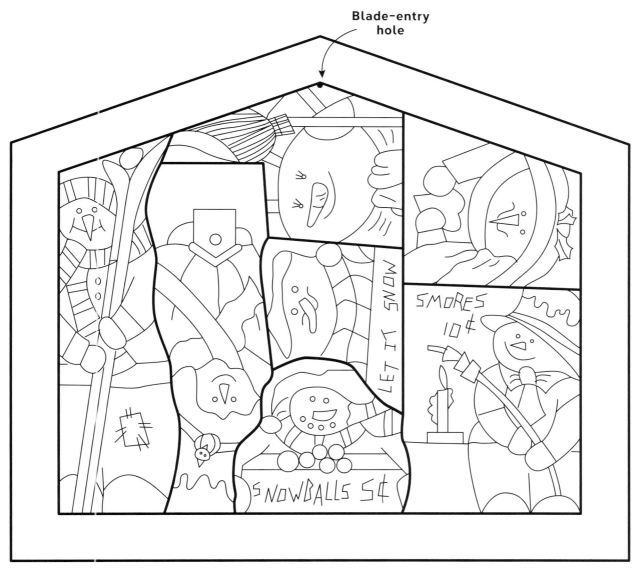

**A Heap of Snowmen Puzzle Pieces, Puzzle Frame, Back Woodburning Pattern (B)**

**A Heap of Snowmen Box Doors (Interior) (A)**

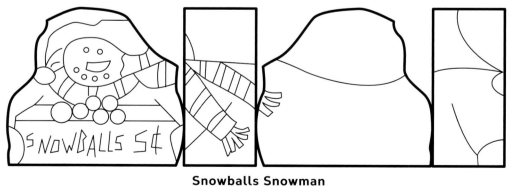

SNOWBALLS 5¢

**Snowballs Snowman**

HERE BE SPARKLEY SNOW

**A Heap of Snowmen Box Interior / Box Bottom (C)**

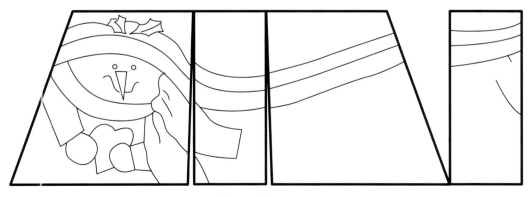

**Heart Snowman**

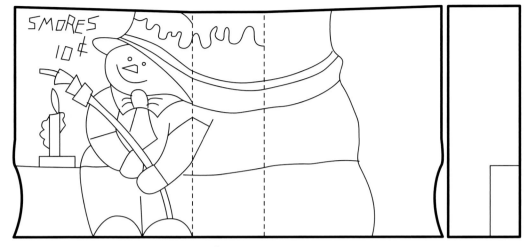

**S'Mores Snowman**

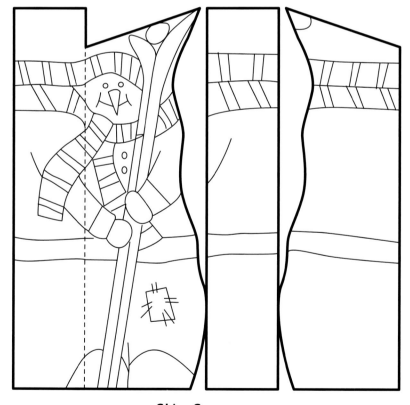

**Skier Snowman**

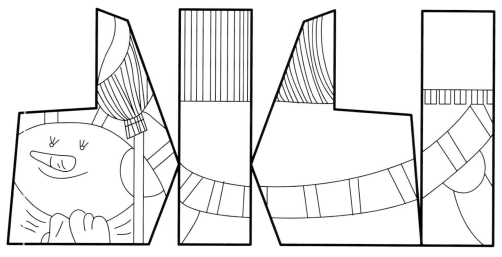

**Snowman with Broom**

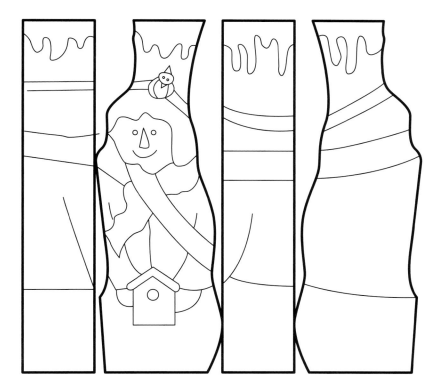

**Birdhouse Snowman**

PROJECT:

# Father Christmas Collection

I designed the Father Christmas Collection puzzle for myself and my family. The woodland Santa came about because I spend a lot of time in our "woods." The garden Santa was in memory of my mom, who was an avid gardener her entire life. The canoe Santa was for my husband, Ken. He was in the Air Force, stationed in Alaska, and canoed the back waters of Alaska hunting and fishing on his time off. The polar bear and snowy owl Santa is special to me. Ken and I were married during his last Alaskan winter in the Air Force, and they signify what to me was Alaska in 1970. The other Santa pieces are just to fill in the gaps.

## MATERIALS:

- Pine, ¼" (6mm) thick: front A, back C, 2 each 6" x 7" (152mm x 178mm)
- Pine, ¾" (19mm) thick: center B, 6" x 7" (152mm x 178mm)
- Acetone or graphite paper
- Wire brads: #19 by 1" (25mm)
- Brass hinges: 4 each ¾" x ¾" (19mm x 19mm)
- Brass-plated hasp: ¾" x 1⅞" (19mm x 48mm)
- Brass screws: 20 each #1 by ⅜" (10mm)
- Stain: Minwax special walnut 224
- Sandpaper: 120 grit
- Tape: clear double-sided
- Acrylic paint

## ALL SANTAS

- **Faces:** Medium flesh[1]
- **Eyes:** Navy blue[1]
- **Eyebrows, hair:** Oyster white[1]
- **Mustaches, beards:** Oyster white[1] shaded with black[1]

## CANOE SANTA

- **Shirt, hood:** Spice brown[1]
- **Shirt, hood trim:** Linen[2]
- **Shirt sleeve trim:** Brown velvet[1]
- **Canoe edges, horse bridle:** Burnt umber[1]
- **Canoe:** Mushroom[2]
- **Gloves, horse head:** Traditional burnt sienna[4]
- **Paddle, horse mane:** Gilded oak[2]
- **Bag:** Black cherry[2]
- **Christmas package:** Metallic Christmas green[2]
- **Package ribbon:** Splendid gold[2]
- **Ball, water:** Blue bayou[1]
- **Ball:** Bright yellow[3]

## GARDEN SANTA

- **Outer robe:** Old ivy[2]
- **Inner robe:** Sage[2]
- **Hood:** Gilded oak[2]
- **Middle trim of robe, hood:** Aspen green[2]
- **Edge trim of robe, inner robe, hood:** Splendid gold[2]
- **Mittens:** Bambi brown[1]
- **Basket:** Spice brown[1]
- **Basket edge, trowel handle:** Burnt umber[1]
- **Seed packets:** Camel[2], Bambi brown[1], linen[2]
- **Trowel:** Metallic gunmetal[2]
- **Redbird:** Tuscan red[4]
- **Birdhouse:** Copen blue[1]
- **Birdhouse roof:** Autumn brown[1]

## TEDDY BEAR SANTA

- **Robe, hood:** Black cherry[2]
- **Robe, hood trim:** Metallic pearl white[2]
- **Gloves:** Hippo gey[1]
- **Teddy bear:** Brown velvet[1]
- **Teddy bear paws, ears:** Mushroom[2]

## WOODLAND SANTA

- **Pants, hood:** Black cherry[2]
- **Robe:** Traditional burnt sienna[4]
- **Shirt:** Thicket[2]
- **Middle trim of robe, hood, belt:** Metallic espresso[2]
- **Edge trim of robe, hood:** Splendid gold[2]
- **Boots, gloves:** Brown velvet[1]
- **Boots trim:** Spice brown[1]
- **Boot soles:** Burnt umber[1]
- **Rabbit:** Mushroom[2]
- **Rabbit ears, nose:** Pink[4]
- **Rabbit tail:** White[1]
- **Carrot:** Bright orange[3]
- **Carrot tip:** Christmas green[1]
- **Bluebird:** Copen blue[1]
- **Redbird:** Tuscan red[4]
- **Bird bills:** Bright yellow[3]
- **Bucket:** Hippo grey[1]
- **Bucket rim:** Metallic gunmetal[2]
- **Food in bucket:** Gilded oak[2]

## POLAR BEAR SANTA

- **Robe:** Copen blue[1]
- **Hood:** Blue heaven[1]
- **Robe, hood trim:** Metallic gunmetal[2]
- **Gloves:** Hippo grey[1]
- **Bag:** Spice brown[1]
- **Bag tie, lining:** Brown velvet[1]

## HOODED SANTA

- **Hood:** Metallic plum[2]
- **Hood edge:** Camel[2]
- **Holly:** Christmas green[1]
- **Holly berries:** Tuscan red[4]

## BOX

- **Rocks:** Medium gray[2] shaded with black[1] and dry-brushed with white[1]
- **Door:** Spice brown[1]
- **Hinges, latch:** Black[1]
- **Door, sign, holly:** Christmas green[1]
- **Holly berries:** Cardinal red[2]
- **Lantern frame, sign frame:** Metallic copper[2]
- **Candle:** Cardinal red[2]
- **Candle frame:** Orange[3]
- **Light rays from candle:** Red[1]
- **Lantern background:** Bright yellow[3]
- **Sign background:** Linen[2]
- **Letters (woodburn outlines):** Splendid gold[2]
- **Snow:** White[1] coated with gems diamond[2] clear glitter paint

1 Delta Ceramcoat
2 FolkArt
3 Apple Barrel
4 DecoArt

**Blade-entry hole**

**Father Christmas Collection Puzzle Pieces, Puzzle Frame, Back Woodburning Pattern (B)**

**Father Christmas Collection Workshop Doors (Interior) (A)**

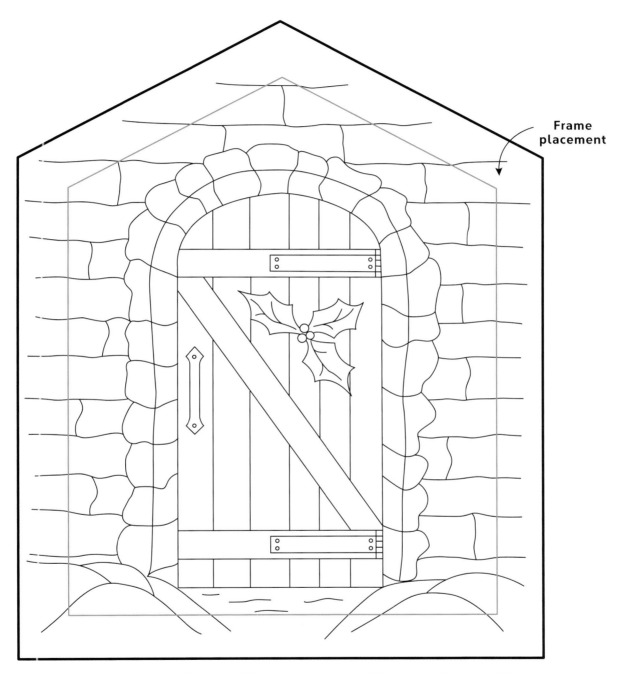

**Frame placement**

**Father Christmas Collection Workshop Interior / Workshop Bottom (C)**

**Father Christmas Collection Workshop Doors (Exterior) (A)**

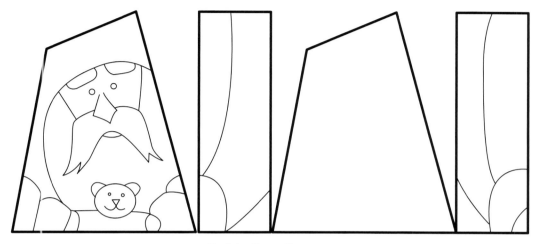

**Teddy Bear Santa**

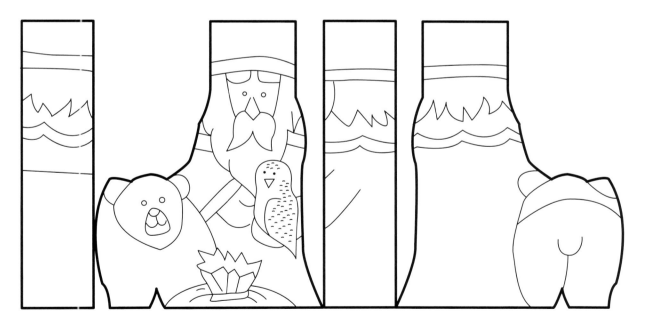

**Polar Bear Santa**

**Garden Santa**

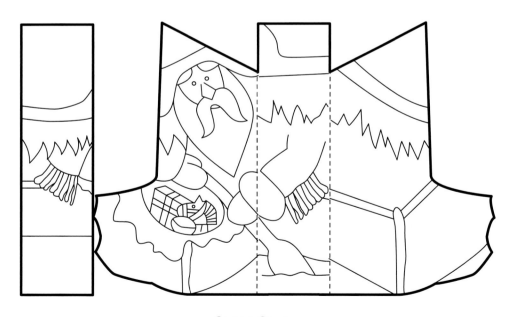

**Canoe Santa**

**Woodland Santa**

**Hooded Santa**

# Index